"*Career Jump!* is a wise and practical guide to aligni: what you want from your life. The book is rich with quizzes, worksheets, and other helpful tools to clarify your career direction, determine where you fit in the world of work, and move forward confidently to set yourself on the right path. I highly recommend *Career Jump!* to everyone who suspects their career may be off track."
C.J. Hayden, author of *Get Hired Now!* **and** *Get Clients Now!*

"I made a couple of major career changes. I quit my job, went on the MasterChef TV program, gave cooking classes, ran a catering business, and wrote a cookbook. I wish I'd had *Career Jump!* at the start of my journey — it would have made it much easier. Dorota's book will give you the nudge you need to start your change. It will help you reflect on and understand what truly matters to you, so that you will not only focus on your goals, but actually enjoy the process."
Bojana Snijders-Nikodijević, author of *The Plan, Prep, Plate Method: Simple Dinners for Busy Families, a former strategy consultant turned professional chef, and MasterChef finalist*

"If you're thinking of changing direction in your professional (and personal) life, look no further than Dorota's book, *Career Jump!* It breaks this possibly daunting prospect into manageable pieces, and gives real-life examples and experiences of a variety of people who made the change. Dorota's style of coaching shines through too — supportive, practical and helping you jump to the next level. I especially liked the exercises, and the models which give structure to the thinking on offer. The spirit of the book is in line with today's shift towards purpose as a measure of fulfillment, instead of pure acquisition. Having made the change myself a decade ago without these tools, I only wish this book had been available then!"
David Beckett, Pitch Coach, founder of *Best3Minutes*, **author of** *Pitch to Win*

"Are you feeling stuck in mid-career misery, exiled to employment ennui, or convinced that occupational opportunity is passing you by? Then Dorota Klop-Sowinska's *Career Jump!: How to Successfully Change Your Professional Path* is definitely for you. Dorota masterfully and methodically guides you through the challenges and complexity of career transition, taking you from where you are to where you want to be –and how to get there. The exercises, prompts and insightful questions of her seven-step process engage; case studies, examples, research findings, and quotes inform and inspire. With *Career Jump!*, you'll identify and build on your values, talents, interests and passion, unlock your life's purpose or true calling, and discover the meaningful work you're meant to do."
Linda A. Janssen, Resilience, Cross-Cultural & Transformative Leadership Coach, Trainer, Speaker; author of *The Emotionally Resilient Expat: Engage, Adapt and Thrive Across Cultures*

"If you want to work in your dream career, not just dream about it, this book is for you. It provides you with diverse tools to help you to carry out the project of transition from your current job to the dream one. Dorota translates psychological theories into practical language, complementing them with plenty of exercises that help you to get to know yourself better. Be prepared: the process of transition will be demanding! Nonetheless, always keep in mind that by the end of the process, you will have attained a happier and more fulfilling life."
Joanna Wencel, Psychologist by education, CRM Specialist by experience

"I have already read tons of self-help books related to self-development and career transition, so I was doubting if I could find anything new in this book. But I did! This book has a lot of exercises and tools that I haven't seen anywhere else. Plus, the vivid stories of Dorota's clients make the book inspiring and motivating to get off your butt and act! I highly recommend it!"
Anna Debinska, Matketing and Sales Leader

CAREER JUMP!

HOW TO SUCCESSFULLY CHANGE YOUR PROFESSIONAL PATH

DOROTA KLOP-SOWIŃSKA

ISBN: 978-90-830073-0-4

DISCLAIMER

The instructions in this book are not intended as a substitute for psychological counseling. If you think you need help, please see a mental health professional. The author and publisher disclaim any responsibility or liability resulting from the actions advocated or discussed in this book. The purchaser of this book assumes the responsibility for the decisions they take during and/or after reading the book, based on the information in the book.

In the interests of preserving client confidentiality, some clients' names and identifying characteristics have been changed, except where permission to use their first and last names has been granted. The scenarios, situations and results are real.

While the author has made every effort to provide accurate information, such as Internet addresses, at the time of publication, neither the author nor the publisher assumes any responsibility for errors or changes that may occur after publication. Further, the author does not assume any responsibility for third-party websites and their contents.

Editor: Anna Rich
Layout: Lisa Hall *lemonberry.com*
Cover Design: Syril Lagapa Pulido *99designs.com*
Diagrams: Cidgem Guven *crocusfield.viewbook.com*
Author photo: Cristina Stoian *cristinastoian.nl*
Illustrations: Samrat Chakraborty *upwork.com*
Proofreading: Rachel Deloughry *lazulimedia.com*

To my beloved daughters, Julia and Sophie,
thank you for endlessly bringing joy and purpose to my life.

CONTENTS

Introduction   Page 11

PART I: The Awakening

Chapter 1: Where are you right now?   Page 23

Chapter 2: How did I get here?   Page 47

Clients' stories: Robert   Page 52

Chapter 3: How Can I Move Forward?   Page 57

PART II: The Career Model

Chapter 4: Introduction to the Career Model Page 77

Chapter 5: Why? Your values   Page 81

Clients' Stories: Vera   Page 96

Chapter 6: How? Your talents   Page 101

Clients' Stories: Marieke   Page 118

Chapter 7: Why? Your life mission   Page 125

Clients' Stories: N.S.   Page 142

Chapter 8: What? Your passions   Page 147

Chapter 9: Where? Your ideal workplace — Page 157

Clients' Stories: Yoli — Page 168

Chapter 10: Who? The right people — Page 175

Clients' Stories: Lisa — Page 180

Chapter 11: Putting the puzzle pieces together — Page 185

Clients' Stories: Amanda — Page 200

PART III: The Transition

Chapter 12: Transition Plan — Page 207

Clients' Stories: Anna — Page 224

Chapter 13: Who really controls your life? — Page 229

Chapter 14: Empowering and Limiting Beliefs — Page 237

Clients' Stories: Kasia — Page 270

Chapter 15: Getting Support — Page 273

Clients' Stories: Catherine — Page 281

Chapter 16: New Habits — Page 285

Chapter 17: Just DoSo! — Page 291

Your Story — Page 292

Bibliography — Page 293

Acknowledgments — Page 294

INTRODUCTION

"Life isn't about finding yourself. Life is about creating yourself."
George Bernard Shaw

My story

My wake-up call came on a warm September morning. I opened my eyes. I tried to look around but I could not move, as there were needles and pipes attached to every part of my body. I wanted to say something but I had a tube in my throat. It was a respirator. After a while, the nurse noticed that I was awake and came over to my bed. She smiled and said "Good morning" in a nice calming tone, then gave me a pen and paper. My hand shaking, I wrote, "What happened?" She told me that the doctor would be with me shortly.

The last thing I remembered was that I had given birth to a beautiful baby girl. There were complications with my placenta, though, so I had to be operated on under full anesthetic. I remember feeling scared and exhausted but I pretended to be calm and relaxed, as I didn't want to take anything away from my husband's experience of that joyful moment. I just asked how long it would take. The doctor assured me that I would be back with my baby and husband within two hours. So when I noticed that it was seven o'clock, I thought it was seven that evening. It turned out to be the morning of the next day. And I was lying in intensive care.

When the doctor finally arrived, he told me that I had had major internal bleeding that they couldn't stop. They needed to perform a second operation. Finally at two o'clock that night, a vascular surgeon arrived. He was the only specialist in Amsterdam who could perform this type of operation. I was given 10 liters of blood — almost twice as much as a full blood transfusion. Thanks to the operation, my womb and my life were saved. I was quiet.

The doctor's account sounded unrealistic: life threatening bleeding, operations, intensive care. Could that be true? But when I finally saw my husband, he started to cry. I thought, "Oh my, it must have been serious."

Luckily all was well with my little girl. She had slept peacefully next to her dad all night through while I was fighting for my life.

I was struck by a couple of signs that clearly showed me that the fact that I was alive and could still have more children in the future was a miracle. To start with, when I asked to talk to the specialist who had performed the operation that had stopped the bleeding, I heard that he had fallen off his bike and broken his arm the following day. When I took my new baby to see my family in Poland, various gynecologists told me that if this had happened there, my womb would have been removed (at best).

Nevertheless, the realization that it was a miracle that I was alive came slowly. As I had been unaware of what was going on under anesthetic, it was as if it had never happened. I felt the consequences in my body but I did not feel them in my heart. Then one day, after a few weeks, it hit me. I was thinking about preparing to go to hospital to deliver my daughter. I remembered sitting, huge-bellied, ironing her tiny clothes. In that moment, I finally made the emotional connection with what had happened. I felt several emotions all at once: sorrow, fear, happiness, relief. Tears ran down my cheeks. Then a further thought hit me: this could have been it. No more dreams to fulfill, no more happy moments with my little girl and my husband. Nothing. While my life was hanging in the balance, I did not see any tunnel of light. I could have slipped away without any consciousness that it was happening. That thought freaked me out but it also changed my life. In difficult moments, when I have to make difficult choices in pursuit of my dreams I think, "You were given a second chance. Don't waste it."

When I chose my first studies at the age of 18, I did not consider what I was good at or what I really liked. I chose to study economics at the best economic university in Poland. At that time, in post-Communist

Poland, it offered new perspectives — "a window" to another world. It also offered good career possibilities, and my mom had studied the same course when she was young. It seemed to tick all the boxes.

I hear a similar story almost every day from friends and from the women I coach. We choose studies because we think they will provide us with a good career and a nice lifestyle. And we think that this will be enough to make us happy. For some, it is. For others, it is not. One day we wake up feeling that something is wrong. I am not happy, I do not like my job, I feel burned out. This signals that it is time for change. It is time to wake up!

I do not regret my initial choice, though. After all, each of my previous decisions brought me to where I am today.

After completing my studies, I finally managed to get a foot in the door of the corporate world, as an office manager. The company was small and growing fast, so I convinced my boss that I would be a greater asset to the finance team. He agreed. My first role was as an accountant, and later I was promoted to finance manager. At work, I met a Dutch man, Mr. Klop. We fell in love and eventually we decided that I would move to the Netherlands. There was one problem, though: I did not want to move without securing a job as I valued my independence. After a few weeks of wondering what to do, I noticed that my company had posted a vacancy for an internal auditor at their HQ in the Netherlands. I had to give it a try! I somehow convinced my future boss that I would be a great asset and he offered me the job. Wow! I was so happy.

Corporate life in Amsterdam was crazy. I spent almost half my time traveling, so it was difficult to make friends and settle down. I did like the job — it involved traveling the world in business class, I earned a good salary, and could afford luxuries like a red Mini Cooper — but a nagging voice within asked, "Is this all there is to my career?" So eventually I gave it up. Many people do not understand why I exchanged a great job for uncertainty, no money (at first), cold-calling. For me, there is just one answer: purpose. I feel that what I do now REALLY has purpose and contributes to something bigger than myself. Even while

I worked in the corporate world, my long-term plan was to become an auditor at the United Nations or a similar institution. I wanted to feel that what I did would benefit others — and not just the shareholders. I wanted to be a part of something with a higher purpose!

After my wake-up call, I decided that I needed a job that I was interested in. And that was not auditing. My passion was psychology.

By the time my husband and I celebrated our first wedding anniversary, I was pregnant. Our apartment was being repainted for the arrival of our baby so we stayed in a B&B. What a great experience! We were tourists in our own city. That weekend, leafing through a psychology magazine, I came across an advertisement for the Academy of Psychotherapy. I went onto their website and subscribed to their newsletter — why, I don't know. I could not have imagined that two years later I would be studying there. It felt out of reach at that time and impossible to realize.

Do you also have dreams that seem unrealistic?

When I finally decided to completely change my career, I wanted to study psychotherapy, with the intention of working with traumatized children. After much thought, I decided to start with a year of studying coaching and counseling. "Before I start a five-year course, I want to find out if this path is for me," I thought. But during that period, I realized a few things about myself. First, I came to understand that I probably was not suited to working with children. I realized that I wanted to work with other women. Secondly, in the first years of my work as a coach/counselor I realized that I much preferred this type of work to psychotherapy. I love to work with my clients on their future rather than be looking into the past. I am still amazed by how it all worked out.

Four years ago, I decided to write a book but I did not do much about it until this year. I had many obstacles and excuses to conquer. The first was that I had three ideas for the book, and I found it difficult to choose one. I started with the idea that I thought would sell well. But every time I sat down to write, a little voice said, "You should be writing something else." Finally, I decided to follow my heart and write this version of my book. Two years ago, just before the birth of my second daughter, the book was almost finished. But I did not manage to finalize it. Soon after she was born, we moved to Mexico. My husband took on a new project for a year. I thought it was a great opportunity, as I wanted to fully enjoy motherhood.

My family and friends know I am very ambitious, so they wondered what my plans were for this year in Mexico. I said I would stay at home with my children and finalize my book. Did I do it? I have to admit that I couldn't put my mind to it. I was busy settling in, helping my older daughter to adapt to her new school, and taking care of my baby. Later, I found a great nanny so I then had the time to work on my book. But I just couldn't bring myself to do it. I was spending time with my Polish girlfriends, taking Spanish lessons, and visiting museums. Looking back, I am convinced that the reason I could not get down to work on my book was that it was not part of my new identity. Before I moved to Mexico, my identity comprised of being a mum, wife, daughter, sister, friend, coach, entrepreneur, and beginner author. My professional identity was strongly present in my daily life and was supported by others. But when we moved to Mexico, I lost the professional part of my identity. One of our primary needs is for our actions to reflect who we believe we are. In other words, our actions should be coherent with our identity, and we will talk more about this later. In Mexico, I did not define myself as coach, entrepreneur and author and I no longer had the professional network of clients and business friends that I had had in Amsterdam.

After a year and a half, and a turbulent decision-making process, we decided to return to Amsterdam. From day one, I planned to resume my coaching business and writing my book. But when I looked at the draft again, I didn't like it at all. So I decided to start all over again.

And I am so happy and proud that you are holding a copy of my book!

I hope that it will help you to realize your own personal and professional dreams, no matter how crazy they seem. Life is too short to spend it doing things you do not want to do!

About this book

Career Jump! is an interactive process I designed in order to help you in the best possible way to find out what you REALLY want to be doing in your professional life. Throughout the book I often use the word "career". I don't mean by this that you need to be climbing the corporate ladder; what I mean is your professional life irrespective of whether you work in academia, in a hospital, corporation, NGO, have your own business or anything else you envision for yourself.

Most of us were brought up by parents whose highest ambition for their kids was a well-paid, decent job, which would set us up for a comfortable life and socially perceived success.

Choosing the right career was not a matter of heart but a matter of a well-calculated, rational decision. But the world changed rapidly at the end of the last century. The globally connected economy, the explosion of a whole new world thanks to the Internet, and the rise of an entrepreneurial spirit has significantly changed the professional landscape. The corporate careers that were so desired two or three decades ago have become golden cages from which we desperately want to escape.

This change has also created enormous growth and increase in the variety of attainable career options. But with the illusion of freedom of choice, the fear of making the wrong decision has emerged. Although we have so many more options than our grandparents and parents ever had, we feel paralyzed before we even take a step.

As societies grew richer, a big shift happened: from well-paid, rationally chosen corporate jobs towards heart-centered, purpose-driven career paths. The further automation of many corporate, administrative functions will push upcoming generations even further towards careers that they are not only skilled in but are meant to do.

We are internally driven towards professions that offer to fulfill our need for meaning and purpose (helping others, making a positive impact) and at the same time, we are pulled by the world's most pressing problems such as poverty, climate change, the conservation of the environment, fighting plastic pollution, human rights and much more.

Many of us have already made the leap towards a second career. But many of you are still undecided, clinging to the old choices and your current career. This book will help you navigate these uncharted waters and will lead you to your new, fulfilling professional path.

The book consists of three parts. The aim of part one is to let you assess where you are at the moment in your life and career. It will also help you understand which steps you took to get there and which steps are necessary to take to go forward and make a change. This part is about answering three big questions: Where am I now? How did I get here? How can I move forward?

Part two is the heart of the book. There, I will take you through a seven-step process in order for you to find out what it is that you really want to be doing. You will discover your core values that rule all your life choices. Without having full knowledge and understanding of them, you will never be able to make lasting choices that make you feel happy and fulfilled. We will shine the light on your unique talents so that you can thrive in whatever you do. I will guide you towards discovering your passions, as only by doing what you love can you fully use your strengths. Then we will go on a quest to uncover your life's mission, because by incorporating your mission into your career you will fulfill your highest needs. Subsequently, based on the above, you will decide which work environment fits you best and with what type of people you want to surround yourself at work. We are social creatures and need others around us. But we are all drawn towards different types of people. You will have a chance to discover who inspires you and which people bring out the best in you. Finally, in the last step of this part, you will put all the pieces of the puzzle together, so that you can clearly see the full picture: your new career.

Once that is ready, in part three, I will guide you through the practical and psychological steps you need to take to make your new career a reality. In this part you will discover what limiting beliefs stop you from realizing your goals, and you will learn how to transform them into empowering beliefs. You will set new goals and a detailed transition plan so that you can reach your new destination. You will also learn how to build your support network so that you can use the help of others, which is a crucial part of ensuring success. And, last but not least, you will also see how to establish new positive habits so that you can take the right actions. So as you can see, the book covers it all!

To inspire you, there are many examples from my own life and from that of my clients who have successfully navigated their own career changes using these tools. This book wouldn't be complete or half as helpful if it were not for the stories of 10 of my clients who were willing to share their career transitions. Robert, Anna, Marieke, Vera, Catherine, N.S. (preferred to remain anonymous), Lisa, Kasia, Yoli and Amanda have written their own stories for you.

Three types of clients/readers

In my coaching practice, I have come across many different types of clients and for the purposes of this book I will define them in the following ways:

1. Clients who say, "I want to change my career, but I do not have a clue what to do next." Very often, it becomes evident that they did know it on a subconscious level. They just didn't know how to get to this information. If you feel this way too, the next part (part 2) is a must-read for you. It will help to influence both the rational and the intuitive parts of your brain, so that you can find out what it is that you want to do next in your professional life.

2. From time to time, I have clients who come to me with many different options for their next career. They just don't know which path to choose. They are full of energy, creative, and love many different things. If you feel that you are this type of person and you already

have some ideas about where to go next, I also strongly recommend that you go through all the chapters in part two. Why? In this section, you will create what I call career "filters" for yourself. They will enable you to make the right choices. Through the exercise of defining these filters it will become clear to you which option(s) is/are the winner(s).

3. It does not happen very often, but once in a while I get a client who knows exactly what she/he wants to do next in their career. The only problem is that they either haven't dared to do it yet and they need a little push, or they need help in making a transition plan. If you are in this group, I still recommend that you go through the second part of the book. The reason you might consider reading it is just to reassure yourself that you are making the right choice. If, however, you are still convinced about your choice and want to act quickly, go directly to part three, where I talk about how to make your plans a reality. We will go through both practical and psychological hurdles that you need to overcome in order to fully enjoy your dream career. So even if you want to skip part two, do NOT skip part three.

I recommend to all readers to read part 3.

Important resources

Next to the various exercises in the book, I have included online resources that will help you on your path. Throughout the book I mention if an additional resource is available, and you will be able to download it at www.dosocoaching.com/careerjump or www.careerjump.nl.

Secondly, I have created a Facebook community where the readers of the book can connect, exchange ideas, network and support each other. Join the group, post your photo with the book and actively participate. https://www.facebook.com/groups/careerjumpbook/

Fasten your seat belt! And off we go!

PART I

The Awakening

CHAPTER ONE

Where are you right now?

"My sun sets to rise again."
Robert Browning

Life changes

There is a reason you are holding this book. It means that you are curious, or that you are not happy with where you are in your career right now. In both cases, I invite you to use this chapter to take stock.

We are constantly busy. We have many roles that we juggle continuously. This book is meant to help you to stop spinning the balls for a moment so that you can reflect on your life and career. What aspects are you happy with? What are you not happy with? Throughout the book, I will ask many questions that will help you to get to know yourself better. By doing this, you will be better equipped to decide on the career that will make you happy.

The train

To explain the typical course of our careers, I often use the metaphor of a train. If you are on a moving train, it is very difficult to get off and change direction. So when do we get off? When the train stops.

It often stops when a major life-changing event occurs: when we become parents, when we reach burnout, when we get sick, when we move abroad, when we are made redundant. So if your train has stopped and you are at the station, take a look around. Do you know where your train was going? Were you happy with the direction in which it was taking you? If yes, great. Get on again and continue the ride. If not, stop! Take your time before you catch the next train. I want this book to be your station. The station where you can figure it all out. And once you have, you can then catch the right train!

Motherhood

I also know from my own experience as a mother, and from that of many of my female friends and clients, that another very positive life-changing event, becoming a mother, can trigger a wake-up call. The moment I became a mother I knew my life had changed forever. It completely altered the hierarchy of the things I considered important in life. It also changed my views on my career. At that time it all came back to purpose. Let me explain. When I first found out that I was pregnant, I immediately decided that I would stay at home with my baby for a year. I didn't want to put my baby into a crèche after three months.

During my maternity leave, I often imagined what it would be like to return to work after a year. I couldn't get my head around the fact that I would be going back to a job that, let's face it, was fine but that's as far as it went. I was thinking, "If I am to put my little baby in a crèche, it cannot be for something I do not fully believe in; I would be busy all day, working on something that was without purpose for me."

Don't get me wrong, I don't mean to be disrespectful or disapproving of women who do go back to work after maternity leave. We all do what we believe is best for ourselves and for our families.

When we become mothers, we take on a new role. A role that comes with many responsibilities. We are responsible for the new life we have created. We are also responsible for setting the best example of what is possible, for our children. I believe that this most important role in our lives forces us to look at ourselves from a different perspective. Forces us to look deep into our own soul and ask: Why am I on this earth?

Have you been asking yourself this question? Yes? Then it is time to look for an answer, my friend.

Moving abroad

Ninety-five percent of my clients have moved abroad. As a result, many of them were forced to look for a new career in their new country. Some of my clients initiated the move themselves, to work in a different country and to broaden their experience of life. Some of them moved to join their foreign partner, while others moved to follow their partner's career.

Whatever the reason for a move abroad, change forces us to look critically at ourselves, our career, our life, and to assess whether we are still satisfied with it or not. It is also a great opportunity to redefine yourself and start something new.

Life satisfaction circle: where are you now in your life?

Although this book is about your career, I want you to have a look at your life as a whole at this point. Our professional life has a huge impact on the other parts of our lives and vice versa.

"Life Circle" (also known as "Circle of Life") is a well-established coaching tool, which is designed to give a helicopter view of how satisfied you are in different areas of your life. For the purpose of this book, I have designed my own version of the "Life Circle". There are ten elements in total: health, self-care, family, friends, career/professional path, money, self-development, spirituality, hobbies and contribution.

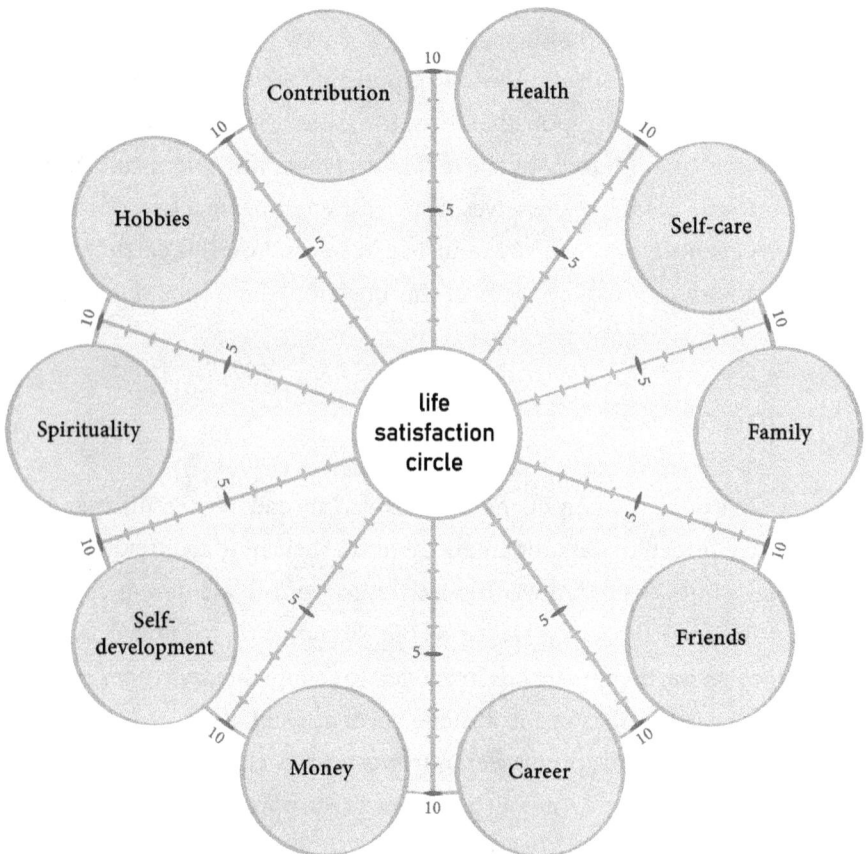

For every element I will ask you to score yourself from one to ten, where one represents a very poor level of satisfaction and ten, the highest level. It is, of course, very difficult to score nines and tens in all aspects, and some aspects will be more heavily weighted than others for you — it is very personal.

I am a huge fan of combining family and career with hobbies, contribution to society, self-development and money — and I make a point of doing this in my own life. But all combinations are possible! It is up to you to decide. After deciding on a score, think about which elements are most important to you and check how you scored on those.

So let's have a look at where you stand on all these elements.

1. Health

It all starts with health. You cannot have a successful, fulfilling career when your health is impaired. And you also probably know from your own experience that stress at work has a major impact on your health. Although we cannot avoid stress completely, we need to know how much we can take and how to charge our batteries again. I have split the health into two parts: the physical health and the mental one. They often go hand in hand, but sometimes there is a split on how we feel mentally and physically. Things such as levels of stress, anxiety, feeling depressed etc. fall under mental health.

So now I want you to give yourself a score from 1 to 10 on the state of your health (separately for mental and physical health). What is the score — and why? Is your work contributing to your score, for better or for worse?

2. Self-care

Self-care is closely related to health. I see self-care as an expression of love towards yourself. If you love yourself, then you are going to take care of yourself. You are going to exercise, eat healthily, and sleep enough.

Self-care is not only about taking care of your body but also about feeding your mind and soul. It is about reading, meditating, spending time in nature. The better you take care of yourself, the better the state of your health.

It is also about respecting yourself and choosing to surround yourself with people who are kind to you. A couple of years ago, I noticed that some friends were causing more negative feelings than positive. Whenever I met a particular friend, my stomach ached and I felt stressed. This friend always made negative comments about me and, more particularly, my new career direction. They were dressed as sweet and caring comments, but I always felt pretty miserable after seeing her. I decided to talk to her about it, to give our relationship a chance, but it didn't work out. So I decided to stop contacting her. I chose my wellbeing and myself above our friendship. It was painful, I have to admit, yet necessary. Nowadays I consciously choose those I spend time with. Are they positive, uplifting people or negative people who drag me down?

Again, score yourself on self-care. How can you improve your self-care? Which people around you make you feel happy about yourself? Which people drag you down?

3. Family

I love my family. I cannot imagine my life without them. For me, my family is the most important aspect of my life. Although I love my work, I know that my family comes first. I am also aware of how fortunate I am · in having the family I do, and extremely grateful for them all, from my grandparents, aunts, uncles and cousins, to my parents, and my husband and daughters. I know that not everyone has the family they wish for. And even if they do, they sometimes do not see them that often.

During our sessions, one of my clients, Anna, realized that although she thought of herself as a career woman, she longed for her parents and siblings who lived far away. As she discovered that family was her number one value, to be truly happy, she needed to go back home and continue her career there.

Ask yourself how happy you are with your family situation. Do you have a loving and supportive partner? Do you see your family as often as you wish? Perhaps you would like to have kids but you are putting it off? Obviously we do not have complete control over all aspects of our lives, but with some we do. It is a matter of becoming aware of what is important to us and making appropriate changes when it is within our power to do that.

You have so much more power than you think!

4. Friends

As an introvert, I have a small circle of friends. The result of moving from Poland to the Netherlands, and then living in Mexico and Brazil, was that my circle of friends often changed. It also made me realize how important friendship is to me. And I have to admit that I do not score as highly as I would like to on this element.

I have noticed that the elements of family and friends often get low scores among my international clients. Why? When they move to a different country, they leave friends and some family members behind. And making new friends takes time. While separated from friends and family, they realize how important these elements are.

Take a look at your own life. How would you score in this aspect? Are you happy with the quality and the quantity of your friendships? Would you like to have more friends, or deeper relationships with some of them? Are your friends supportive?

5. Career/Professional path

As you know by now, for years I wasn't really happy with my career. And I didn't even realize it at first. Dissatisfaction with career is a top reason that brings my clients to work with me. So, in this book, I will talk in great depth about how to become satisfied with your career and about the elements that increase or decrease your happiness in it. At the end of this chapter, take the quiz. It will show you which aspects of your career you are happy with, and which you are less than happy with. This will help you to rate the career element.

6. Money

Money is obviously very tightly connected to career. One of the main purposes of working is to earn money! In fact, for some it's the only point. Think about your financial situation. How happy are you with it? What are your financial ambitions? Are you reaching them? Money is also a means of realizing some of your dreams.

Rate your finances from 1 to 10. Now think about why you gave yourself this score.

7. Self-development

I can say without hesitation that self-development is my passion if not obsession. When I moved out of my parents' apartment, I rented a cute, tiny apartment of no more than 20m2, in the center of Warsaw, just opposite Empik bookshop, which was my favorite store. After work or during the weekend, I would sit for hours at the self-development, psychology, and spirituality section. I spent lots of money on books. When I moved to Amsterdam, my biggest collection was not clothes, shoes, or bags, but self-development books. I still think it is amazing that I have been able to make a career of my passion.

Nowadays I still read tons of books, but I also develop myself through training, coaching, networking, and inspiring events. I am a true believer in the power of coaching, so I have a coach myself. My coach helps me to go beyond my limitations. I also love to listen to the stories of inspiring people. They help me to develop myself, to be inspired and, by extension, to inspire my clients.

Self-development is also a common quality of many of my clients. They are hungry to learn new things; they are hungry to develop themselves. And they are willing to invest in themselves. I believe that investing in yourself is one of the best ways to invest. It is a clear sign of self-care too.

Self-development means that you are willing to continuously improve yourself and to step out of your comfort zone. And as you are holding this book, you are already on that path!

So how do you score on self-development? Do you feel you do enough to reach beyond your limitations? Do you have a coach? Do you invest in your own education?

8. Spirituality

I have a particular relationship with spirituality. On one hand, I perceive myself as rational, with both feet firmly on the ground. On the other hand, I am very intuitive; I just know certain things before even being told them. I practiced Buddhist meditation for years, and I love yoga. I see spirituality as listening to your intuition. Some call it the voice of God, the Universe, or your Inner Wisdom but irrespective of the definition, I believe that spirituality means having a relationship with your higher Self. For me, this is a comforting thought. It makes me feel safe and taken care of. I have also noticed that when I go against my inner wisdom I get into trouble. At many times in my life, I have seen that I am protected when I listen to this voice.

For me, spirituality is also about gratitude, about taking time to acknowledge all the good things that have happened to me and feeling grateful for them.

A couple of months ago, I got stomach flu. My husband took our daughters out to play so that I could rest. I was alone at home, lying in bed, when I suddenly felt a lump in my right breast. My hair stood on end, and I felt a sharp pain in my stomach.

The following months were extremely stressful. I had to undergo various health checks like ultrasound, mammography, and a biopsy. It was very scary time on one hand but on the other, a time of the highest clarity — clarity about what is really important in my life. But I have also come to the realization that the true moments of happiness are the little moments — like playing outside in the sunshine with our daughters and dog. The feeling of gratitude was what made me feel really happy; feeling grateful that I am able to do little things. I realized that I was even grateful that I could put the dishes in the dishwasher — something that I usually hated.

Is spirituality important to you? Do you feel you have a connection with your higher Self? Do you feel grateful for the life that you have? How do you score on this?

9. Hobbies

I have to admit that I am not the best at keeping up with my hobbies. That said, one of my former hobbies took over completely, first growing into a passion and finally becoming my career. To have a balanced life, I know I want to spend time on my other hobbies, like yoga, cooking and knitting, but there's still room for improvement. This is my lowest score on the life satisfaction circle.

From my work with clients, I know that hobbies reveal potential prospects for a passionate career. So it is important to spend time developing them. Of course, some hobbies are meant to stay that way — just as hobbies.

What score do you give yourself for this element? Do you have hobbies? If so, do you spend enough time developing them?

10. Contribution

The highest form of fulfillment comes from contributing. How do you do this? By sharing, by helping and supporting others.

We all contribute to some extent. We contribute by raising our kids, by working. But we all want to contribute in other ways too. We want to contribute in the way that matters to us. When I was working in my previous career, I was also making a contribution. Being an auditor meant that I was responsible for detecting where the processes were faulty and how they could be improved. So I was definitely contributing. However, I wasn't satisfied with the level and the subject of my contribution. When I changed my career and became a coach, I finally felt that I was contributing in the way I wanted. I was helping people to improve the quality of their lives. And I felt it mattered. I felt it was important. It is all down to how you feel about the importance and relevance of your contribution. Do you feel proud?

Recently I realized that my purpose had grown and needed my attention again. It was time to revise my contribution. While I was meditating in a group of 600 business owners at an event, I had an amazing vision. You know my story by now, so you know where it is coming from. I saw dark-skinned women wearing white turbans, with large pregnant bellies. I saw laughing children running around them. I saw green hills, and the air was vibrating from the heat. I saw myself sitting among these women, talking to them. At this moment, I realized my life had a further purpose. It is my purpose and my duty to help women in developing countries to survive childbirth, just as I had survived mine. My life was hanging by a thread, but I was sent back to earth to make sure these children had mothers. This is why I have linked this book with my new mission in life.

For every book sold, one Janma, a Clean Birth Kit in a Purse will be purchased, ONE LIFE SAVED. Janma kits provide the sanitary tools and instructions to help women in resource-poor areas survive their deliveries without infection. The kits are produced by the globally renowned company, ayzh — www.ayzh.com, founded by Zubaida Bai.

What is the brick you want to contribute to building a better world? I know you might think: Who am I to help others? I don't have a spectacular story. That doesn't matter! What matters is that you are willing to help. And with this book, you will find your unique way of contributing.

What are your scores? Which elements scored highest and which, lowest? How do you feel about that?

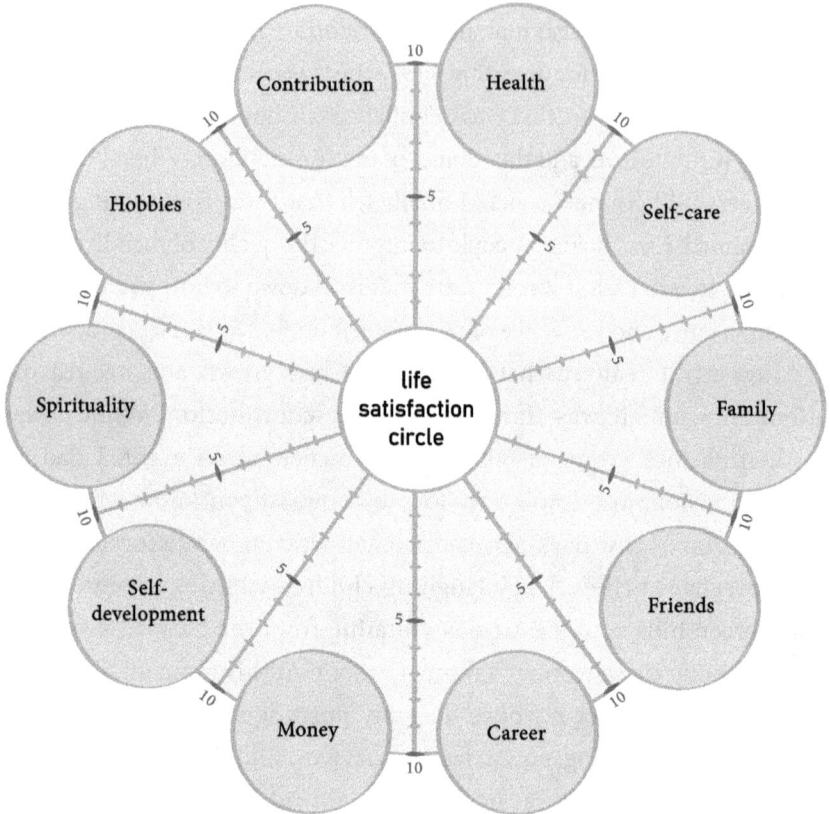

Where are you now in your career?

"What a man can be, he must be."
Abraham Maslow

When I was 17, while I was at high school, I took my first job to earn money for my holidays with friends. I stood in the pouring rain handing out leaflets about electric toothbrushes.

After a couple of days of this simple work, I had earned enough money for my holidays. But that was just a job, not a career.

A few years later, after I had graduated from university, I looked for a company that would hire me so I could start my real career. After a couple of months of searching, I finally got one. I was ambitious and I worked very hard. Soon I was promoted from office manager to accountant and then to finance manager. Later on, I moved to the Netherlands and continued my career there. I had a dream career. I was traveling around the world, doing work I liked, had a great boss and team, a good salary and a fancy car. And that was my brilliant career.

After my first daughter was born, the house of cards that was my career collapsed. All the years spent on building my career, all the effort and energy I put into additional studies all became irrelevant. I no longer wanted my career. I wanted something else. Back then, I didn't know exactly what it was, but I know now. I wanted to have a calling. I wanted to contribute, and to feel that my work had true meaning. And I found it.

Two years after quitting my career and being a stay-at-home mum, I started my professional path in the coaching business. In the past few years I have helped more than 100 people to discover their own professional path. I am able to combine my unique gift of listening with my passion for human development. My life's mission is to help others to build their own extraordinary, meaningful professional paths. This is my calling.

Maslow's hierarchy of needs

About 90 percent of my clients come to me with the same issue. They discover that they have outgrown their career and feel the need to do something else — something that is bigger than them.

So how does this happen? Why do we no longer want the career we so carefully designed for ourselves over the years?

Do you remember hearing of Abraham Maslow's pyramid of needs? Maslow was an American psychologist who came up with the psychological theory of how and what motivates us to reach our full potential. He described his theory in detail in his book *Hierarchy of Needs: A Theory of Human Motivation*. Initially he came up with five needs that drive our psychological development: physiological, safety, love, esteem and self-actualization. Later he added three more: cognitive, aesthetic and transcendental needs.

Here are some examples of each:

» Physiological needs like sleep, food, shelter, drink
» Safety needs like security, protection, order, rules
» Belonging and love needs: love, family, relationships, belonging
» Esteem needs: respect, achievement, status, reputation
» Cognitive needs: knowledge
» Aesthetic needs like beauty, art, nature, music
» Self-actualization needs: personal growth, self-development, self-perfection
» Transcendental needs: helping others, spiritual needs.

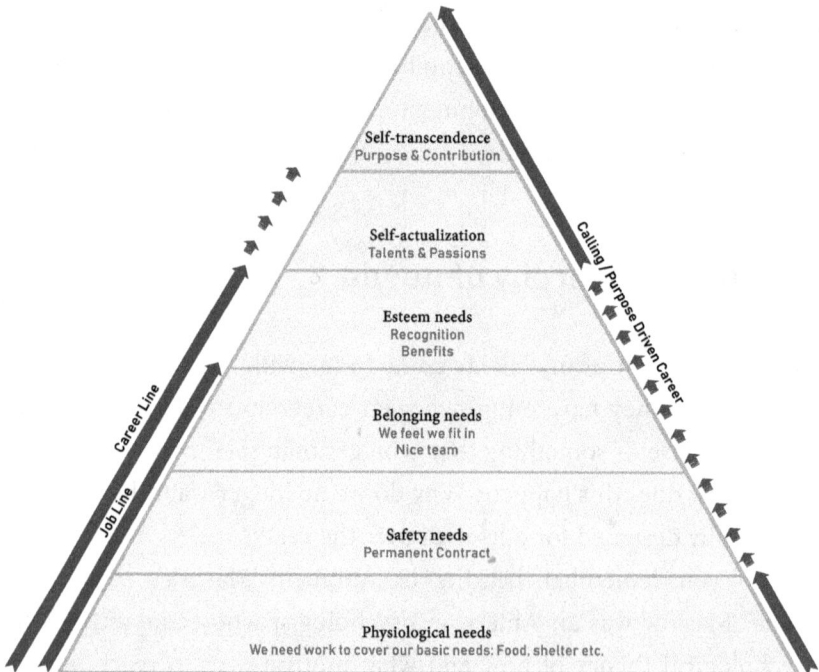

Self-transcendence
Purpose & Contribution

Self-actualization
Talents & Passions

Esteem needs
Recognition
Benefits

Belonging needs
We feel we fit in
Nice team

Safety needs
Permanent Contract

Physiological needs
We need work to cover our basic needs: Food, shelter etc.

Career Line
Job Line
Calling / Purpose Driven Career

We only aspire to achieving a higher need once the previous one(s) have been met. This theory also holds that it is our true nature to want to develop further and further.

Our needs & professional path

For the purposes of this book, I will focus on physiological, safety, love, esteem, self-actualization and self-transcendence needs and link them to the professional path.

I often hear from my clients (and I have experienced this myself) that they feel guilty for wanting more. They have a career that many of their family members or friends would die for, but they just don't want it any longer. They ask me, "How can I be so spoilt?"

But as the theory shows, our feelings have nothing to do with being spoilt; they have everything to do with an immense urge to develop ourselves, to help others and to make an impact.

Maslow's theory of needs can be perfectly applied to demonstrate the development of our professional path (as I showed earlier in my own example).

Job level

When we have a job, we are mainly motivated by these three basic needs:

1. Physiological needs

Your primary motivation for getting a job is to provide for your basic needs. You need a job to buy food and pay the bills.

2. Safety needs

Once you have paid the bills, you start to look further. You want a job that gives you a feeling of security. You want a permanent contract; you want to feel safe in your workplace.

3. Belonging needs

Once the two basics are covered, you start to look for the social aspect. You notice that it is important to have a good boss and a nice team around you. You want to work in a place where you feel you belong and feel accepted.

Career level

Once all the above needs are met, you are ready for the next level: career.

4. Esteem needs

At this level, your need for success and recognition comes into play. You want to feel recognized by your boss and others for your achievements. You want to feel that you are successful. This level is also intrinsically connected to status. We crave the things that demonstrate status, like a fancy job title or a company car. We want to prove to ourselves and others that we matter. Many of our family members and friends may be envious of our thriving career.

Although it is in our nature to develop, many of us stay at this level Why? Because achieving the higher need of self-actualization requires the right environment, an open mind and a determined character.

If you look at extremely successful people, who have fully accomplished that level, you notice that many of them don't stop there. Look at the examples of Bill Gates and Richard Branson. What did they do when they accomplished that level? They started to give back. They started to help others. And they did that because our true nature is to develop ourselves further. And we can do that by contributing to others.

A calling

This level is about combining our talents, passions and purpose. Some might argue that this can be also part of our career. Yes, it could be. But I want to make a clear distinction between the focus on achievement and status at career level, and the focus on contribution at the level of a calling. And I know many people who have reached the top level while meeting all the needs of the lower levels at the same time.

5. Self-actualization needs

The last two levels (self-actualization and self-transcendence) are my favorite levels. When we combine them, we do not have a job or career any longer, we have a calling. This is what I strive for every day, and what many of my clients consciously or subconsciously desire. At this level, magic happens.

Self-actualization is the level at which we are able to express ourselves through our talents and apply them to the areas we are passionate about.

Self-actualization means doing work that is based on our core strengths. We all have unique talents, strengths or gifts that we are born with. But we do not always use them. In the corporate world, there is a huge drive to continuously improve our weaknesses, rather than focusing on our strengths. But in doing this, we often lack the energy to keep focusing on our core talents. Only by striving to perfect our strengths can we experience a state of "flow". Flow, as described by another great psychologist, Mihály Csíkszentmihályi, is a mental state in which we are so immersed in an activity that we lose track of time and place.

6. Self-transcendence

Self-transcendence needs are about fulfilling our higher purpose through contribution to others. We want to leave a legacy, we want to reach beyond ourselves and help others grow. In whatever capacity or form, we feel the need to use our gifts not only to make our own lives better but also to better the lives of other people or creatures, or the environment. This level is about having an impact and about truly contributing. This is the level where we transcend our own needs.

A couple of words on guilt, needs & society

As you can see, our psyche works in such a way that we move to each successive level only once the needs at the present level are met, one by one. We are all at different levels. To free yourself of guilt, you need to identify which level of Maslow's pyramid you are on, and that of those closest to you. People who are on the lower levels of the pyramid will generally have a hard time understanding why you need more from life.

As societies grow wealthier, I think each successive generation moves up the Maslow scale. When you look at your parents or grandparents, you realize that they were less concerned about whether their work was fulfilling their passions and more focused on just earning a living. When I talk to people of my grandparents' or sometimes even of my parents' generations, they have trouble understanding exactly what it is that I do. They tend to say something like, "Ah, so you're helping your clients to get a new job, right? You're helping them with their CV, and to find job offers." When I say, "Yes, this can be part of the process, but the biggest part of my work lies in figuring out what it is that they want to be doing," they fail to understand why they don't know what they want to do. They keep asking, "They just want to get well-paid work, right?" When I say, "Well, money is very often NOT the biggest motivator," I lose them. Generally, they just cannot comprehend it.

Our societies have developed to the extent that more and more of us want something else other than just a decent job and a paycheck. It is a natural progression that we cannot stop. Our nature drives us further. We cannot feel guilty about that.

Back to you!

Here are a couple of questions and steps to help you figure out where you are.

1. Where do you see yourself on the pyramid?

   _____

   _____

2. Which needs are being met in your current work?

   _____

   _____

3. Do you feel the need to go higher?

   _____

   _____

4. What do you have now: a job, career or calling?

   _____

   _____

5. Where do you want to go from there?

   _____

   _____

In an ideal world, you would go from having a job to having a career and then pursuing your calling or life's mission. But life is often imperfect. Be aware that it is very difficult to remain at the top while the other needs are not being met. So if you are fulfilling your life's mission but it is not paying your bills, it is okay to defer that mission while you find ways to meet your more basic needs.

Career quiz: Are you satisfied with your career?

Just the fact that you have picked up this book suggests that you are not entirely happy with your career. The reasons for that vary from one person to the next.

In this part of the book, I invite you to look at the different elements of your career in order to locate the pain. So take out pen and paper and write down your answers to the following questions.

1. On Sunday evenings I feel:
    A. Excited to go to work the next day.
    B. Neither excited nor nervous. It's just business as usual.
    C. I have a pain in my stomach, and I feel like crying and calling in sick.

2. The relationship with my boss can be best described as:
    A. Great, my boss is very supportive, has trust in me and I feel I get the best out of myself thanks to him/her.
    B. Lukewarm. She/he lets me do my thing but is rarely involved in my development.
    C. Bad. My boss is a real .... (fill in the word that comes to mind). We are in conflict.

3. My relationship with my colleague(s) is:
    A. An example of great teamwork. Although there are some misunderstandings, we communicate effectively to solve any problems.
    B. Generally difficult. I can find a common language with a couple of them but with several others there is a lack of cooperation.
    C. Hell on earth! I feel misunderstood by most of my colleagues and I do not understand them.

4. The atmosphere in the office is usually:
    A. Really good. People cooperate with each other and are friendly. I feel I can express my opinions.

B. Neither bad nor good.

C. Terrible! People do not communicate with each other. There are many underlying conflicts.

5. My day-to-day work is:
    A. Exciting. I really like what I do.
    B. Sometimes I like what I do, but at other times it is boring and the day drags.
    C. Boring! I really dislike what I do and I can't wait for the day to finish.

6. The way I feel about my job is:
    A. I am really proud of what I do.
    B. It is just a job.
    C. I feel embarrassed when I tell others what I do.

7. I often fantasize about:
    A. How can I further grow my career in my current area of expertise?
    B. How to get a new job a.s.a.p.?!
    C. Doing something completely different to what I am doing.

8. The way I'd describe my work is:
    A. An expression of my talents, mission and values.
    B. A decent job that pay the bills.
    C. Far from my intended path — how did I get here? It crushes my individuality and makes me feel like a loser. I employ my weaknesses more often than my talents.

9. The money that I earn from this job:
    A. Provides me with all I need. It supports my lifestyle; I have enough money to pursue my other hobbies, and to save every month.
    B. Provides me with a paycheck that covers most of my needs. But I won't be able to continue my current lifestyle on this paycheck alone.
    C. My salary is well below what I call a decent standard of living.

10. The stress level at my job is:

    A. Easily manageable. Every now and then, there are situations that cause me stress, but I have supportive colleagues and several effective ways of releasing tension.

    B. Moderate. I have more stressful situations than I would like. It is still manageable, though.

    C. Help! Every day is stressful. I can't cope any longer.

11. My career path is:

    A. Crystal clear. My current job fits in well with it.

    B. A bit foggy. I think I know where I am going but it is not as clear as I would like it to be.

    C. Career path? What's that?

12. Does my career support the work-life balance I want?

    A. Definitely! I manage the demands of my work and family very well in this career.

    B. Somehow! My career allows me decent work-life balance if I plan well.

    C. No way! It doesn't allow me to spend enough time with my family and this creates constant stress.

13. In my field, I would be described as:

    A. An expert. I am really passionate about it.

    B. An expert — but I am not really excited about this field.

    C. I couldn't care less!

14. If I were to quit my job tomorrow...

    A. I would know exactly what to do next.

    B. I would need some time to figure out my next move, but I am reasonably confident I would manage.

    C. I would feel completely lost.

Results

Count how many times you selected A, B or C. which one did you select most often?

Answer A [   ]   Answer B [   ]   Answer C [   ]

You have chosen answer A most of the time.

Congratulations! It seems you have the perfect career, but...

It looks as if your current career ticks most boxes. But please have a closer look at the questions and your answers to them. Check which areas of your work scored highest and which need improvement.

In the areas that could be improved, come up with a short-term plan to directly increase your satisfaction with your job. It is likely that you need to change only a few elements to fully thrive in your career.

Be aware that not all elements have the same importance for everyone. So even if you have a positive score, but your work is stressing you out completely, seriously consider whether you should stay where you are now.

You have chosen answer B most of the time.

Hmm. It seems that you have a suitable career, but there are several items that need to be improved in order for you to be fully satisfied with it. It is time to take charge of your career.

Based on the answers you gave, analyze what is going well and what isn't. Is it related to your boss, your colleagues, the content of your job, or something else?

After you have analyzed which areas need improvement, decide whether it is possible to make changes that would allow you to stay where you are and yet feel satisfied. Read the book carefully to see how you can improve the weaker elements of your career.

You have chosen mostly Cs.

Oh my! Where do we start? Time for some serious changes! It looks as if you are ready for a major career change. But first, analyze the main things you are unhappy about. Is it your boss, your colleagues, the content of your job or the stress levels? Whatever it is, it seems it is time for a change. Your life is too precious! Use this book as a guide to help you to make the right changes.

CHAPTER TWO

How did I get here?

*"The best thing about the past is that it shows you
what not to bring into the future."*
Unknown

"The jobs I have had so far 'just happened'. I didn't actively pursue a particular career or dream. It has all been okay but I don't feel that I have chosen to live my life this way. I would like to regain control."

This quote is from the initial questionnaire that Anna, one of my clients, completed, but it is the story I hear from almost every client. It also happened to me. I took the first job opportunity that came my way, as I wanted to start working as quickly as possible after my studies.

Most of us do not consciously choose our career path. We fall into it. We pursue any opportunities that arise without asking ourselves where they will take us. And I have become more and more certain that we cannot blame ourselves for that. When I look back on my time at secondary school, I see that a small proportion of students knew exactly what they wanted to study and the career they wanted after that. But the majority of us didn't have a clue.

In the first group, one guy wanted to become a movie director, another wanted to be a journalist, and yet another wanted to be a pilot.

They had a very clear vision for their future. And they set about realizing their plan very consciously and deliberately. The rest of us struggled.

In the end, my motivation for choosing to study economics was not that I really wanted to become a businesswoman but that at that time, in post-Communist Poland, it offered new perspectives — "a window" to another world. It also offered good career possibilities, my mom had studied the same course when she was young and I would get to hang around with cool guys. My school didn't offer any support in making decisions about the specific curriculum choice. The majority of the teenagers in the second group, of which I was part, had relatively good grades. Some may have been better at math; others, at languages or history, but for the rest, we just had average grades and ambitions. And I think that in many cases, this is where it goes wrong.

At the age of 17, when you are choosing what to do after high school, you have generally lost sight of your childhood dreams of who you wanted to be. Then, if you are competent at all your subjects, the range of choices is huge, so the decision is often determined by chance or, as in my case, by poor motives. Thirdly, you are not offered support from those who know what questions to ask to guide you. And finally, at that age, you are not really focused on boring adulthood. You just want to have fun.

So how did you get to where you are now? What led you to your current career?

When Elisabeth was a little girl, she dreamt of becoming a vet. She loved animals. But her father thought it was a stupid idea, an unrealistic one, a young child's dream, not to be taken seriously. He had a better plan for his daughter. He wanted her to get a well-paid job that would provide her with a secure life. He wanted her to become a lawyer. So she enrolled for a law degree, graduated with honors and became a very successful corporate lawyer. Although she performed very well at work, getting promotion after promotion, deep inside she knew she was not happy with her job.

I hear many similar stories from my clients. With the best of intentions, our parents generally want one thing for us: to graduate with a degree that will give us a good, secure job, so that we can lead a comfortable life.

When we are young, our talents and true nature are still intact and we have a great connection with our inner self. As we grow older, we consciously and unconsciously start to adopt new strategies. I remember that as a child I once told my mum that I wanted to be a hairdresser, but in her opinion, this was not the right profession for her daughter. She definitely had higher ambitions for me.

The issue is not so much that we learn that there is something "wrong" with certain professions, but in the fact that we get a clear message that our own choices — what we want — is not good enough. As a result, we learn to distrust our inner voice, and we learn to say the right things in order to please others. So we choose jobs that offer a comfortable lifestyle.

Recently, I was shocked when one of the mothers at the playground said she already knew that her daughter would have to be an accountant because the job offers such great earning potential.

As young children, it is in our nature to please others (mainly our parents) to get their attention because we cannot survive without their care. The thing is that when we grow up, we cannot behave like a helpless child any longer; we are responsible for our actions. We do not need to live up to any expectations besides our own.

When my clients start discussing what they wanted to become when they were young, I rarely hear any mention of professions such as accountancy, law or banking. Much more often, they talk about becoming vets, doctors, teachers, dancers, actresses, even garbage collectors. But as a result of the influence of the outside world, including our nearest and dearest, who want the best for us, we choose a career we do not even like because we consider it a sensible choice.

Then when I ask many of my clients, "What do YOU want now?" the answer is, "I don't know!" Their intuition is silent, as they learnt that no matter what they have to say, no one listens anyway, so why bother? Their intuition, their inner voice, is in hiding because it felt betrayed.

Exercise: Who was I supposed to be?

In their book, *I Could Do Anything, If I Only Knew What It Was: How to Discover What You Really Want and How to Get It*[1], authors Barbara Sher and Barbara Smith recommend that we go through the exercise of asking ourselves what the important people in our lives wanted us to become. This helps us to recognize the impact they still have on our lives. We can then ask ourselves if we want to set ourselves free from these "out-of-date" external expectations. It gets even more interesting when we realize that our parents expected contradictory things from us. For example, your father may have expected you to be a good housewife and to take care of your children, while your mother expected you to become a successful surgeon.

Now try to remember what your parents or other people close to you (older brother, sister, grandparents, aunts, uncles) wanted for and expected of you. What did they say about your future?

It is important to know that we start to develop our identity by mirroring. This means we listen to what others say about us and internalize it, which forms our perceptions of ourselves. So if everyone around you said, "She is such a sweet, cheerful girl," it becomes a self-fulfilling prophecy. Any behavior that contradicts the image of a sweet, cheerful girl is automatically perceived as incorrect and is suppressed while behavior that is in keeping with the image of a sweet girl is reinforced.

Now answer these questions:

What did others expect me to become?

_____

_____

What did others expect of me in general?

_____

_____

---

1   PERMISSION granted — see Permissions page

What did others say about me when I was young?

_____

_____

What did I want to become at 7, 12 and 18 years old?

_____

_____

What was the reaction of my environment to this (supportive or unsupportive)?

_____

_____

Who had the biggest impact on my study and career decisions?

_____

_____

What are my thoughts about it now?

_____

_____

One of my clients shared that she always studied hard and got the best grades at school and university and then performed better than her colleagues at work as she thought this was what her father expected from her. When she was in her early thirties, her father told her, "The only thing I want for you is for you to be happy." She was speechless. All those years she had tried to please her father, and he just wanted her to be happy in her own way. That's it!

The main point of this book is to give you (back) the steering wheel of your life — to make you aware of the patterns, both positive and negative, that are shaping your life — so that you can make conscious decisions in line with what you want to achieve. I want you to start believing that the past does not define your future. You can change and redefine your future right now. US life coach and motivational speaker Gabby Bernstein says it beautifully: "_You are the dreamer of your dream._"

Clients' stories

Robert

"You can't process everything simply by thinking it through. But by following your curiosity, in time, you might just discover what motivates you."

I used to work in fundraising, advising international NGOs on how to grow their income. My career was moving at a pace. I was finally getting recognition and promotions. But on a personal level, things weren't great. My health in particular was suffering. It was an interesting situation; from an external perspective, it seemed as if I was going through a brilliant period in my career, but on a personal level, I was questioning it, partly because of my health, but also partly because I wasn't enjoying the work anymore. I knew I needed to change my career; I just didn't know which direction to take.

I met with the company director and told him that I wanted to leave my profession — not just my job, or the organization, but my profession. I loved the organization. I loved its mission and the way it impacted people's lives around the world. I found that part very rewarding, and it's what kept me there for so long. But after 20 years in the development sector, working towards this single purpose alone was no longer enough. Ninety percent of my work took place in front of a computer, and on a personal level I found this immensely frustrating. I knew that if I wanted to stay healthy and inspired, I needed to dramatically change my career and my lifestyle.

The company director didn't want to let me go that easily. He suggested that it would be best to talk to a career coach before making such a huge life decision. I just wanted to move on, but he pushed me to take the time to ask myself if this really was something I wanted. And I am glad he did.

I knew what I didn't enjoy doing day to day, but I didn't have as much clarity on what I did like. When I discussed it with friends and family, I really did not know how to answer the simplest questions, like, "What are you good at?" or 'What do you love doing most?" I learnt something from that process, and that was that it's okay to start with a negative. Everyone tells you to focus on what you like, but my advice would be to reflect on what you don't like first. Ask yourself, "What don't I like about my current profession?" It sounds pessimistic but it's not really, because you can then start to reframe it. So if you start with a negative by saying something like, "I don't like sitting in front of a computer all day," it can prompt you to challenge yourself with a question like, "How can I dramatically reduce the amount of time I spend in front of the computer?" and then take the time to explore your ideas, big and small.

The main question I wanted to find the answer to was whether my profession still challenged me, motivated me and inspired me, and whether it supported the fullness of my personal ambitions and the lifestyle I wanted.

The conclusion I reached through coaching was that it did not. I realized that if I wanted to reignite my zest for life and stay on top of my health, I would need to make big changes to both my career and my lifestyle.

When I started the coaching process, I thought it would be great having a coach who would tell me what to do. But of course it doesn't work that way. You have to delve into yourself, follow your curiosity, and nurture your ideas.

The most difficult part of the process was asking the little questions that I had never actually asked myself. I don't think very many people do — they realize that they are not happy, but they rarely ask themselves questions like, "What excites me?", "What gets me thinking?" or "What makes me smile?"

The coaching process was immensely valuable to me. The session I remember best was when Dorota asked me to bring photos of the things that were important to me. I brought photos from my past, from the present, and some of my imagined future. I still remember which photos I selected. It helped me to realize the things that are dearest to me, and that change was possible.

The "Life Mission" exercise (page 131) was fascinating. Dorota helped me to pull together a range of answers to diverse questions that we had explored. These ideas were then compiled into a mission statement. This process really helped me to find direction. It was clear from the exercise that the main components of my focus were health, family, and lifestyle. Meaningful work was still important, but not if it was at the expense of the other key areas. The coaching helped me realize that in order to satisfy my dreams, I needed to carve my own path. A path outside of employment, a path towards entrepreneurship.

Another important part of the coaching process was finding out which of my skills were transferable. I really needed some help in discovering that. The questions and discussions about my skills were difficult — I felt like I just didn't know what my strengths were. But the "Strengths Finder" (page 102) test was very helpful in identifying my strengths — and then my skills and talents in turn. I really liked the approach of looking not only at hard skills but also at my personal qualities.

I am often quite an impulsive person. But at the age of 38, given the significance of the potential consequences of a mid-life career change, I realized the value of using coaching to take stock of the past, and to ask those difficult questions about the future before embarking on anything new.

People often talk about finding your life purpose; I have never liked that phrase, because to me it somehow implies that there is a single purpose that awaits us. Humans are more complex than that. I believe that there are multiple paths people can take within their life to find fulfillment, motivation and happiness, but sometimes we need to stop for a second, assess our priorities, refocus our attention and redirect our efforts. And for me, that's where coaching can help.

I feel that people sometimes get stuck as they fall into the trap of thinking that they need to figure out the exact direction they want to take. To my mind, it's much better to follow your natural curiosity, to experiment with different ideas. You can't process everything simply by thinking it through. But by following your curiosity, in time, you might just discover what motivates you.

By the end of the coaching process, I was even more convinced that I wanted to move on from my career. I knew that I was ready to start exploring various business ideas. Some of them took off, others didn't. And it was okay — I was exercising patience and allowing myself to experiment. Through this process, I got closer to finding out what I enjoyed most.

I now run a small chocolate factory in Valencia www.tigerandbean.com, manufacturing chocolate bars and chocolate drinks made with tiger nut extract. It didn't happen overnight. There was no epiphany. I moved to Spain in search of a better lifestyle for myself and my family, and started working on several business ideas. A combination of curiosity and continually asking myself the question "What if?" eventually led me to chocolate.

One of my daughters is lactose intolerant. She didn't really enjoy soya or rice milk chocolate, so after discovering the wonders of locally grown tiger nuts in Valencia, I thought, "What if we used tiger nut milk when making a lactose- and dairy-free chocolate?" I then went on to develop a gluten-free tiger nut and chocolate drink mix. It started off as a bit of fun. The tiger nut chocolate products tasted great. People loved them, and kept coming back for more. Then what started out in our kitchen expanded into a purpose-built shipping container that housed our first micro-factory!

It took almost a year of studying the world of chocolate, while juggling other things, before I felt sufficiently equipped to officially dive in. I started with just one machine in my kitchen, then another and another, slowly building it up. It got to a point when I was spending 30–40% of my working hours on chocolate. At this point, I realized I loved every minute of it, and wanted more. Making chocolate challenged me, inspired me, motivated me, and gave me the lifestyle I was looking for — a lifestyle centered around family, friends and food.

I love working in my chocolate factory. Every day is different. The future is, of course, uncertain — but that in itself inspires and motivates me.

Another aspect that I love about running a small company is that you can take it in many directions based on what works and what doesn't. I love the creativity of this process. I also love working with different people every day. And, best of all, I love being surrounded by chocolate!

Running a chocolate factory is complex; it requires that you wear many different hats. The complexity can be intimidating at times, but one thing that I have learnt is that managing complexity is one of my greatest strengths. If I hadn't moved on from my previous career, I may never have discovered that. Sometimes we need to step out of our existing profession to discover our greatest strengths.

My advice to anyone who has fallen somewhat out of love with their job, or even their profession, is that it's okay to feel frustrated. Frustration can be a powerful emotion that helps motivate you, as it was in my case. Use your frustration to come up with new ideas and a new direction, and to power change, even if that change is incremental. And crucially, talk to someone like Dorota — someone impartial, someone who can ask the difficult questions. They won't give you the answers, but they know what it takes to find a new direction.

Chapter Three

How Can I Move Forward?

"Look at the word responsibility — 'response-ability' — the ability to choose your response. Highly proactive people recognize that responsibility. They do not blame circumstances, conditions, or conditioning of their behavior. Their behavior is a product of their own conscious choices, based on values, rather than a product of their condition based on feeling."
Stephen Covey

In the previous chapters, you have focused on the past and present. You have assessed where you stand in your career and how you got there. Now you have reached an important point, if you are ready to take the next step: to make a decision about what you want to do in your professional life from now on. This is a thrilling and, for most people, scary moment as it is a step into the unknown.

Do you remember the metaphor of the moving train? During the process of reading and digesting the content of this book you will decide which train you want to catch next. For some, the image of a train journey is useful. For others, it may be more appropriate to visualize the change as a jump from a plane or as breaking through a wall. Either way, I want to help you to realize that it is your responsibility. No doubt your knee-jerk reaction is to agree with me, just as many of my clients do, nodding and saying, "Of course I am responsible for my life and my decisions." But when I ask why they are not yet on the right train, they respond with things like, "Oh, I just don't have enough money to start new studies" or "I am too old to change my career" or "My partner would not approve of my new choice." Well, let me tell you that these kinds of answers do not indicate that you are taking full responsibility for your own life. Rather, they are a sign of blaming others, or resigning yourself to fate or external circumstances; they are excuses for avoiding action.

Taking full responsibility for your life and career means that you make a promise to yourself and others to do everything possible to reach your desired goal, then duly act on your promise. Of course, by everything possible, I mean within ethical boundaries and the values you carry. By stating your intention for your next move to yourself and others, you are already making the change, as it is then substantial in your own mind and in the minds of those around you. Every time you repeat this promise, you are a step closer to making the change; you are making it more difficult to return to your current career.

I am far from perfect myself! I am a good example of avoiding taking responsibility for my own actions. For example, writing this book was much more difficult than I thought it would be when I started, and finalizing it was particularly difficult. Months passed, and when people asked how my book project was coming along, I would answer that I was still working on it. My biggest issue was time. I had a list of excuses that prevented me from finalizing my book: raising my kids, running my coaching business, and doing all sorts of things that we all use as justifications or excuses for not reaching our goals. There was always something that prevented me from writing. Often yet another week would pass without me working on my book.

Then I heard myself complaining to my husband that I did not have time. I realized that I was putting myself in the role of victim and not taking responsibility for finalizing my book. I realized that what I often preach to my clients was something I was not taking responsibility for myself. It had to change; I wanted to change it! I realized that I had much more time than I actually thought. Previously, I told myself that I needed a couple of free hours to write and the right environment for me to feel inspired to write. I started to realize that if I sustained this belief, it would take at least 10 years to finalize my book. Obviously, I didn't want to wait that long. So my first step was to get rid of this belief. I replaced it with a new, more empowering one: "I will write every day irrespective of the place and time." That helped me enormously. So I started to write every day, especially during the evenings when the kids were sleeping. Previously, I would switch on a Netflix series and spend my evening relaxing on the couch. This was my other limiting belief: "After a day's work, I need to watch Netflix to relax." I found that working on my book for most of the evening gave me a great sense of satisfaction and accomplishment. And some evenings, I still watched my favorite series after my writing time. On such occasions, I did not feel that I had wasted yet another evening.

If you feel that you are at the crossroads now, you have a choice. You can go back to your old life without changing a thing. You can keep complaining that you do not like your job, your boss is blocking your promotion or your colleagues are stupid. But you can also make a decision that you will take responsibility for your own happiness and future and take action. Do not think that you need to start writing your resignation letter immediately. The actions can be baby steps at first, to allow you to get used to the idea and to gain confidence. This might even be the best strategy at first. By taking smaller, more feasible steps, you can prove to yourself that you are able to do what you promised yourself. This will fuel your motivation to take bigger and bigger steps. You will become confident in your power to make things happen.

One of my clients, Marie, is great at taking baby steps. Marie had known for a long time that she was not happy with her career. Then finally she told herself: "Enough!" and she sent me an email. We started to work together. The first months were pretty difficult for her — and for me too. Although Marie said that she was committed every time we spoke, she actually acted as if she was not. She often turned up for our sessions unprepared and when I asked her what she would like to work on during a particular session, she always said that she had hoped that I would come up with a topic. But after a while, a big shift happened during the coaching. At one of our sessions, Marie told me that she had learned to kite surf at the age of 43 despite a huge fear of water. When she revealed how she prepared for it, it was clear that she was a master at taking small but consistent steps to achieve her goals. I also noticed that although she was not always prepared for her sessions, she never canceled or rescheduled, which is often the case with other clients. She was extremely committed. During our coaching sessions it became clear to her that initially she had avoided taking responsibility as she had felt that the task was overwhelming. So we split the process into much smaller steps so that she could feel in control. From that moment, she took off and claimed full responsibility for her career change.

Now think about the situations in which you take full control and responsibility for your actions. Think about why you take responsibility in those situations. How do you feel when you take ownership? What exactly are you doing in this situation? How do you act? And how do you feel? It is extremely important that you become fully aware of your patterns. You need to know exactly how and why you have succeeded. Then you can apply the same approach to other areas of your life and work. We will discuss this further in Chapter Six, the chapter on talent. The way we succeed is directly related to our strengths. Marie discovered that her main strengths were determination and consistency in reaching her goals. This was her way of succeeding; yours may be different.

The four elements necessary to start any process

Soil represents having the right plan to start with. In other words, soil is about laying strong foundations for your ultimate goal. It is about getting the basics right in order to begin moving forward. So, for example, if your goal is to start your own company, you need to be aware of all the basic requirements for starting a company, like the need for a business plan, knowledge of how tax works and so on. If you do not have a firm foundation, your plant will eventually die — even if you fill your days with hundreds of actions and have the right support.

Every project, every challenging goal you set for yourself starts by planting a seed. A seed can be very small, but it is concrete. When I started my coaching business in 2010, I planted a lot of seeds: I sent emails to potential clients, I talked to people about my plans, I attended networking events, I organized free workshops. After some time, I noticed that some of them were starting to sprout. I nourished them and gave them my full attention. Some sprouted much later. Others just died a silent death. I noticed that my seeds needed four things: water, sun, soil and love.

Water represents action. I needed to take concrete steps to allow my seeds to sprout and to develop into beautiful flowers. I needed to set goals and then execute them with strong determination. Without execution, nothing would happen. Without actions, your seed will never sprout; it will die. Some of my clients hope that we will figure it all out together during our coaching sessions, and that this will be the biggest part of the action. But they soon find out that in order to reach their goals, they need to start watering their sprouts; they need to take action themselves.

> *"If you let your learning lead to knowledge, you become a fool.*
> *If you let your learning lead to action you become wealthy."*
> Jim Rohn

Sun represents the support you need from the right people. I am sure I wouldn't be where I am now with my business and I would not be writing this book if not for the support and belief of my husband. On many occasions, he had much more belief in me than I had in myself. Whenever I was down, he would tell me how great I am and how proud he is of me. Support from those closest to us is of the utmost importance. I have also noticed that if you intend to make a big change in your life, you need to stay away from people who drag you down. Often their behavior is based on underlying jealousy or lack of understanding. It sounds drastic and dramatic but it really is necessary. If you cannot immediately get rid of all those who have a negative effect, at least keep your early ideas from them. Share them only with people who believe in you and support you. I talk more about the support of others in Chapter Fifteen "Getting Support".

Love represents the attention you give your goal. This may sound abstract but it is fundamental to success. Love is seeking inspiration from others who have done the same. Love is brainstorming your idea. Love is believing that it will work out. Love is visualizing your goal on a daily basis. Love is listening to your intuition and acting on it.

Take the example of my goal of writing this book. I sat down to write it (water), I had the support of my family and friends (sun), I found out all the basics of getting a book published and I read lots of other people's books (soil). And then beyond that, I visualized myself standing on stage during my book promotion event, holding a copy of the book. And even more importantly, I have come to believe that I can do it (love).

So what is your seed? How do you envision taking care of it, making sure that it has all that it needs? What is your water, sun, soil and love? Do you already have an idea? If not, do not worry. This book is about finding out how to plant your seed and grow it into to a beautiful blooming tree.

Commitment

Before we dive deeper into this book, I want to ask you to make a commitment to yourself: a commitment to read this book from beginning to end and, even more importantly, that you will do the exercises that are included. It will be challenging and you will sometimes feel that you want to lay it aside and go back to your old self and your old life. Only by committing to and following the process will you be able to use the book to get to where you want to go. But although it can show you the way and even open the door for you, you need to walk the path yourself. You need to take the necessary steps.

If, at times, you feel like throwing this book into the corner, first read Vera's story on page 96 — it will help you to get back on track.

Exercise: Timeline — Look into the future

"The best way to predict the future is to create it."
Abraham Lincoln

When I was thinking of my own career transition from auditor to coach/counselor, one of my main worries was that I was too old to start something new, as I was 33. When I finally made the decision to start my new studies in coaching and counseling, it turned out that I was the youngest in the group of 15. There were two other women around my age but the rest of the group was older. Some of the men were around 60. I had two thoughts at that time: first, how happy I was that I had taken the decision to make the change then, rather than 10 years later, and secondly, how brave of these people to follow their dreams regardless of their age.

Lesson learnt: IT IS NEVER TOO LATE TO MAKE A CHANGE.

What do I want to accomplish by then?

My Age:	My Age:	My Age:	My Age:
NOW – fill in date:	1 Year from NOW – fill in date:	3 Years from NOW – fill in date:	5 Years from NOW – fill in date:

How can I move forward?

My Age:

10 Years from NOW –
fill in date:

My Age:

20 Years from NOW –
fill in date:

My Age:

30 Years from NOW –
fill in date:

When we look at our decisions from a different angle, taking a long-term perspective, it can shed a totally new and refreshing light on how we judge those decisions. For example, you might think that new studies or a transition to your new career may take a long time, perhaps a couple of years. But if you look at it from the perspective of how much time you will still have to enjoy your new career as opposed to continuing something that you dislike, the initial time investment you need to make the change will suddenly feel much shorter.

To make the point, I do the same exercise with all my clients who start my career coaching program: I ask them to visualize us having a chat with each other in the same room, one year later. I ask them the question: "What has happened in your life and career in the year that has passed?" After that, we go further ahead in time to 3, 5, 10, 20, 30 years on and repeat the same question.

As most of my clients are between 28 and 45 years old, this exercise always creates a strong realization that they still have many years ahead of them. And that they had better invest their time and energy in something that they really enjoy doing!

Below you will find a list of questions to help you to complete the exercise.

Use them as a guide for every period of 1, 3, 5, 10, 20 years from now. Remember that it is about your ideal life, so do not limit yourself. This exercise is not about being realistic; this exercise is about your dreams and desires. So allow your mind to run free and your imagination to flow. The best way to do this exercise is to get a friend to ask you the questions. If possible, take a very big piece of paper and make a copy of the drawing above.

1. Imagine that we meet in 1, 3, 5… years from now. Ideally, what has happened in your life in the meantime, both professionally and privately?

_____

_____

2. What are you doing? What is your profession?

_____

_____

3. Where are you doing it?

_____

_____

4. With whom are you doing it?

_____

_____

5. Who else is there with you in your life?

_____

_____

6. What would you regret not having done in this period of life?

_____

_____

7. If this whole exercise is a book about your life and every period is a chapter, what title would you give to each chapter? What is the essence of each chapter?

_____

_____

8. What is the title of the book? What is the essence of your life?

_____

_____

Try another more creative form of the exercise

This is a great way to use the right part of your brain, where the emotions are locked. Our right brain works on images, not words, which is the reason you need to do the following.

Take a big piece of paper, draw a line like the one in the example above and write down the main keywords that have come out of this exercise. Go through your favorite magazines and look for the pictures that inspire you and that you could use as visuals to complete a book about your life.

It is best to hang it where you will see it. Then keep adding new pictures whenever you spot something inspiring or that fits the picture.

Now take a moment to think about how this new perspective helps you to take the right decision. Write it down.

On the other side of the river

"Dreams don't work unless you do."
John C. Maxwell

I know that right now you might still be thinking:

I cannot do it.

I need to be responsible.

I need to be realistic.

I need to play it safe.

I do not know what I want to do next in my career.

I do not know how to change my career.

And these thoughts are making you feel:

Frustrated

Sad

Angry

Unworthy

Incapable

Trapped

Helpless

Overwhelmed

So as a result you:

Spin in circles.

Start and stop, start and stop, start and stop.

Search the internet forever.

Complain endlessly to your friends.

Read tons of books.

And as a result YOU DO NOT TAKE ACTION.

You are still standing on the same side of the river. You see the water in front of you. It might be crystal clear, it might be shallow, deep, muddy, dark. On the other side of the river there is a new future waiting for you.

The future where you think:

I respect myself.

I am happy.

I have talent.

I have passions.

I am making a contribution.

I matter.

I live once.

I have dreams.

These thoughts will make you feel:

Vulnerable

Needed

Loved

Giving

Appreciated

Strong

In control

This positive state will cause you to take the right action. You will:

Take a decision.

Make a plan.

Work on your mindset.

Take action.

Find positive people.

BREAKTHROUGH!

I am sure that as you are reading this you are saying to yourself: "Yes, I want to be there!" And let me tell you, this is all in your hands now. You *can* reach the other side of the river. If I could do it, you can do it too. This book is your lifeboat to get you safely to the other side of the river. But you are the one who needs to steer and row the boat in the right direction. The book can be a great tool. But the boat cannot get to the other side by itself. It needs you. It needs the captain! It needs your commitment!

There might be times when you want to return to the old bank. You might feel that the boat is tilting strongly in that direction. And there might be people pulling you and the boat back. It might get stormy, cold and dark. But hear this. This is normal! Everyone goes through that. The adventures you experience along the way are what make this journey so exciting and make you a wiser person. You cannot protect yourself against all the risks. But I am not telling you this so that you do not set foot on the boat. I just want you to be prepared. As Gabrielle Bernstein said, "Obstacles are the detours in the right direction."

And since you have now been presented with both sides of the river, would you really consider staying on the unfulfilling one for the rest of your life? Seriously? How old are you? Are you 30, 40, 45, 50? Work out how many years of your working life you have left. Let's assume you will retire at the age of 65 — though the retirement age will probably be shifted to 70 in many countries. You still have somewhere between 20 and 35 years of work. You might not even be half way! Do you want to continue doing something you do not enjoy for the next 30 years, then wake up at 65, regretting that you wasted your career because you were afraid? Or would you prefer to start all over and find a career that will fulfill your values, talents, passions and life mission, so that you can lead a happy, fulfilled life, feeling proud that you did not give up on yourself and your dreams?

Ready for part 2?

So if you are ready, I invite you to continue to the second part of the book, the heart of the book. In it, you will define the most important "filters" through which you will look into new career opportunities.

So are you ready to step onto the boat? I really hope you are! I believe in you.

PART II

The Career Model

Chapter Four

Introduction to the Career Model

*"The secret of change is to focus all of your energy,
not on fighting the old, but on building the new."*
Socrates

In this part, I introduce you to the *Career Model*, the heart of the book. In it, you will have to do most of the work! That is, unless you already know what it is that you want to do and are just looking for confirmation. The Career Model consists of six elements — I like to call them filters — through which you will look at your career.
The filters will help you to:

» Find out more about yourself
» See why you are not yet fully satisfied in your career
» Enable you to discover the career paths that suit you best
» Choose your career path, once you have generated a couple of different ideas.

The six elements, the filters, are:

✓ Your values	✓ Your passions
✓ Your talents	✓ Your favorite working environment
✓ Your life mission	✓ Your favorite type of people

Each of these elements answers a BIG question you need to ask yourself in order to reinvent your career and take the next step.

Your values and life mission answer the question "WHY?". Why do you do the work you do? What is your big "WHY?" that, once connected to your career, will make you feel alive, satisfied and fulfilled?

When you look at your talents, you will answer the question "HOW?". How do you want to perform your work? Which of your talents do you want to employ in your everyday life and career? Which talents help you to thrive?

In search of your passions, you will answer the question "WHAT?". What things do you love doing, what are your hobbies, what makes you come alive?

While considering your favorite work environment, you will answer the question "WHERE?". Where do you want to work, in which country, which environment, sector, company? Here you will define your perfect working conditions and environment.

Last but not least, you will answer the question "WHO?". Who do you want to connect with? Who do you admire, who motivates you?

Each chapter in this part of the book covers one of these elements. After each chapter, I will ask you to sum up what you have learned about yourself and your career path. In the last chapter you will combine all the elements to see what career path you want to pursue. Make sure you spend enough time on this part of the book. Please be aware that you will not necessarily have an idea immediately. For some of my clients, it takes 6 to 12 months to figure it out. So take your time, do not rush it, but stay on top of it. If you cannot do it alone, give me a call or ask a friend for help. You can download the Career Model at www.dosocoaching.com/careerjump.

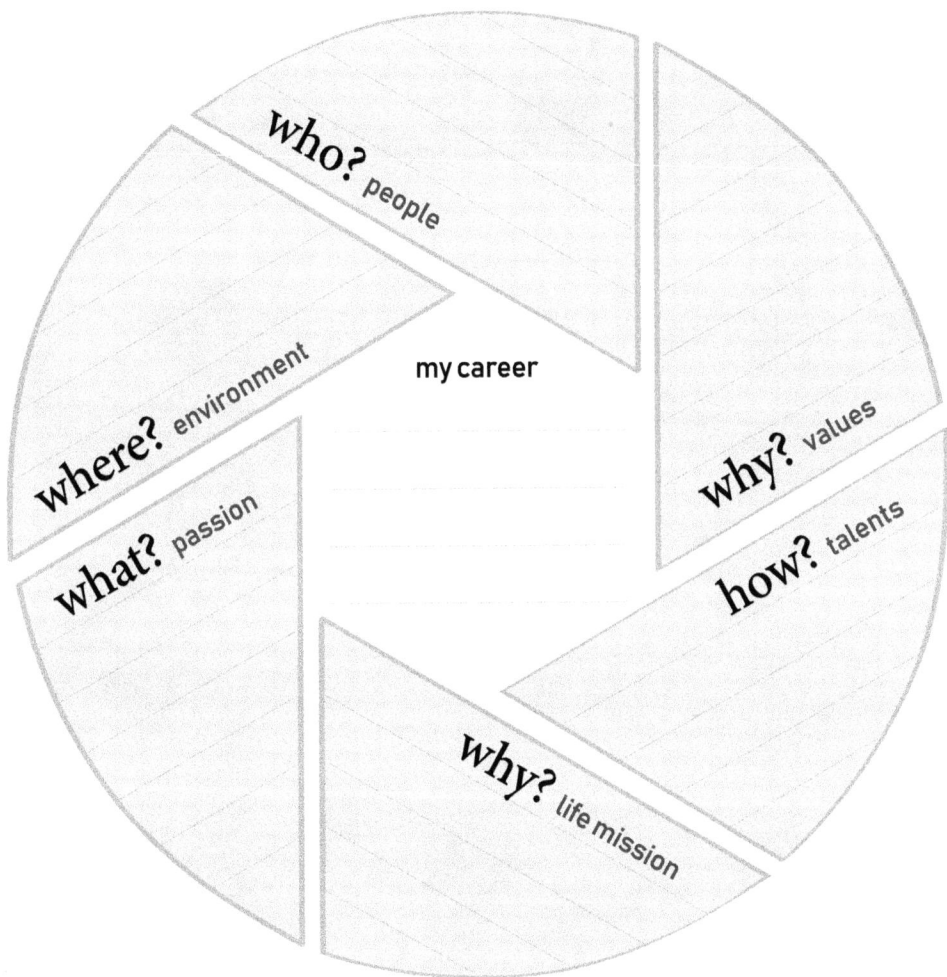

who? people

where? environment

what? passion

why? values

how? talents

why? life mission

my career

Chapter Five

Why? Your values

"Your beliefs become your thoughts,
Your thoughts become your words,
Your words become your actions,
Your actions become your habits,
Your habits become your values,
Your values become your destiny."
Mahatma Gandhi

What are values?

Simply put, values are the things we regard as most important in our lives. We inherit them from our parents, teachers, community and culture. I believe that some values are woven into our personalities. Only by knowing your values and making changes that are in line with them will you set yourself on a successful path that leads to happiness and fulfillment. Take for example my value of inner peace. I am by nature introverted, so for me to function well and be happy, I need time alone to recharge my batteries. Someone who is extroverted is not likely to regard this value as such a priority.

Why are values so important?

Values lie deep within us. They form part of our identity. We have a huge need for consistency between who we are and the way we behave. What does that mean? It means that if you are to be satisfied in your life and work, your actions need to be aligned with your values.

You can't make a decision and expect that it will have a positive effect if you do not know what your values are!

When my clients say they are not happy with their work, the first area we look at is their values. And it holds true every time: they are not happy in their work because one of their top values is not being honored, either by them or by their work environment.

Self-discovery

The first time anyone asked me about my values was during my coaching and counseling studies. Guess what? I didn't have a clue. I had previously associated the concept of values with things like religion and patriotism.

From a list of 30 values, I was asked to choose my top five. After a lot of indecision, I came up with family, loyalty, honesty, responsibility and self-development. I noticed that my values were quite different from those of the other students in my group. After some consideration and discussion with Dutch colleagues, I discovered that mine were the reflection of a very different cultural background. I recognized my Polish roots in the values of loyalty and responsibility in particular. During the communist era, loyalty to your group was very important. You could not survive without others. We relied on our network (often made up of neighbors) to a great extent for things that sound incredible now, like letting us know when products such as bananas or meat had arrived in the supermarket! I realized that my values were very group-focused and those of my Dutch peers, much more individual-focused.

After a couple of years of further soul searching, I came up with a slightly different set of values: family, inner peace, self-development, meaningful work and contribution. This does not mean that the values I came up with during my studies are no longer my values. They are still deeply embedded, but my personal development means that my more recent choices reflect what I want to become. To fully evolve into that person, I need to honor these values.

My values in practice

So how do I honor my values? By identifying actions in my daily life that are in line with my values and consistently choosing those actions.

Family

What does this value mean to me? I prioritize this value above all others — family comes first. This means that I work part-time to have time to be present for my daughters. This also means that I regularly spend quality time with my mum, father and sister, who live in Poland. And it means that I spend quality time with my husband.

Inner peace

This is huge for me. Over the years I have noticed patterns in my energy levels and in the way I felt during the day. I noticed that whenever I was in a busy environment, I felt drained, tired and irritated.

I learned to honor this value: I discovered that if I did not cultivate inner peace, I would not have energy to do the other things I wanted to do. Honoring this value means that I take weekly me-time seriously. It means that whenever I am in a busy, crowded place I take time to slow down afterwards. This value means that I say no to others when my energy levels are low.

Self-development

I was a serious little girl who loved to read and learn. I still do. As it happens, I also love to read about self-development. I think the work I do now as a coach is the best way to honor this value. My main function as a coach is to help others to develop and grow. But I cannot do this well if I do not grow constantly myself. I keep looking for ways of "improving" myself. Recently, I hired a business coach to help me with my company. In the past, I worked with a public speaking coach who prepared me for an event at which I gave a speech to few hundred women.

This value means that I spend time, money and energy on developing myself through reading, participating in courses, events and classes. It means that I face my limitations and seek help internally and externally to overcome them.

Meaningful work / Contribution

These values led me to change my career. Even at the outset of my career, I knew that I was not going to do that work for the rest of my life. You have already read that I wanted to help, to contribute. At first I was like a child in the mist, completely lost. I thought I wanted to become a psychotherapist, specializing in helping children heal from traumas. I still believe that helping innocent children who have been the victims of an abusive parent and/or environment is one of the most beautiful contributions you could make in life. But during my studies, and especially once I started to coach people, I discovered that it is not my path. I discovered that I prefer to work with adults — and I am better at it.

The value of contribution means that I help others by coaching them, but also by giving my time, money and energy to causes I believe in. This is the reason I decided to link the proceeds of this book to a good cause: securing safe childbirth for women who live in poor and challenging environments. You read all about it in Chapter Seven.

Conflicting values

If you feel unhappy and unfulfilled in your life or career, I recommend that you look for clues in your value system. Almost certainly, you will find that two or more of your values are in conflict.

One of my clients, an expat, first came to me when she was thinking of moving from the Netherlands to another country as she had been offered a top position there. She didn't know what to do. On one hand she wanted it, but on the other, she felt something was wrong. She felt torn apart. Her top values were career and family.

But when we dove deeper into understanding her values, we discovered that her number one value was family. As an expat, she had been living far from her family for a few years, but she realized that she couldn't do it any longer.

She understood that although career was important to her, family held first place. She rejected the offer and moved back to her home country. When I spoke to her a couple of years later, she said it was one of the best decisions she had ever made.

Unhappiness can arise when we are in an environment with values that are in conflict with ours. The more I work with my clients, the more I see that it happens often. Although organizations come up with beautiful sounding value statements, in reality they often don't walk their talk.

Be aware

Before I published this book, I asked a couple of people to read it and give me feedback. What emerged was that, for several of them, discovering their values was the hardest step in the process. For some, it was difficult because they felt it was a crucial point and they wanted to do a perfect job. Others struggled with the selection of the top 3 based on their conflict situations (in Step 2).

If you find that it is hard for you too, firstly, welcome to the club! Secondly, do not let yourself be stopped by it. Remember that "Done is better than perfect", and that you can always go back to this exercise and adapt it, should you feel the need to do so.

Exercise: Discover your values

Do you know your values? If yes, great! If not, don't worry. I will help you. There are different ways to find out what your values are. Take a look at the list of values below, then follow the steps.

List of core values

Adventure	Happiness	Pleasure
Art	Health	Privacy
Beauty	Honesty	Reputation
Career	Independence	Respect
Comfort	Influence	Safety
Compassion	Inner peace	Self-confidence
Contribution	Justice	Self-development
Control	Kindness	Spirituality
Creativity	Knowledge	Stability
Excellence	Leadership	Success
Faith	Love	Trust
Family	Loyalty	Truth
Freedom	Nature	Wealth
Friendship	Peace	Wisdom

Step 1

From the above list, please select ten values that are the most important in your life, the ones you use in your life as guidance and the ones that demonstrate who you are as a person. Think about the meaning of every value. Where do they come from: your parents, family, country? It would be best if you could do this exercise with a friend. If this is possible, then describe the definition of each value to your friend. You will probably notice that you very often have different definitions of many values.

1. _____   6. _____
2. _____   7. _____
3. _____   8. _____
4. _____   9. _____
5. _____   10. _____

Step 2

The second method is to analyze difficult situations in your life. Think back to these situations, specifically when you had to make a decision and you didn't know what to do. The difficulty of making a decision is very often caused by an internal conflict of values.

Now take your time to think of five difficult situations in your life and explore the conflicting values.

> » Were you happy with the decision you made?
> » What does it tell you about the hierarchy of your values?
> » Which value won at that time and what was the outcome?

Conflict 1	Value 1	Value 2
Conflict 2	Value 1	Value 2
Conflict 3	Value 1	Value 2
Conflict 4	Value 1	Value 2
Conflict 5	Value 1	Value 2

Based on these insights and the list of values above, please select your five most important values.

1. _____
2. _____
3. _____
4. _____
5. _____

Step 3

Now it is time to select your top three values. Once you do that, keep in mind that this does not mean that the others stop existing. Think about the three values you couldn't live without, or, to put it more positively, which three values bring you the most joy and fulfillment in your life.

1. _____
2. _____
3. _____

Step 4

Once you are clear about your value system, answer the following questions:

» Do you honor your values at the moment in your career?
» Is your workplace nourishing or damaging your values?
» Score your top three values from 1 to 10 in accordance with how well you think you incorporate these in your career.
» What does it mean in practice for you to live in line with your values?
» What do you need to do to realign your values and your career?

Step 5

Discuss your top three values with your loved ones if you can. Do your values match or clash with those of your husband, wife, partner, mother, father or best friend?

This is a very powerful — and possibly confrontational — way to really get to know what is important to the people close to you. Investing in this will definitely improve your relationships.

Work your values

I believe that values are the most important thing in life, so we need to become fully aware of them. More than that, though, we need to live accordingly. Our core values show us what is important to us and can also point to what is missing in our life.

In this section, we focus on the values that are specific to work. In other words, things that you consider important in your professional life.

If your core values guide your life, then work values should guide your career. What we like and dislike at work becomes clearer over our working lives. And what we dislike becomes particularly visible.

Exercise: Work values

Step 1

Score 1 — On a scale of 1 (low) to 5 (high), rate how well the statement for each value matches your values in general. This will test the importance of a given value for you.

Score 2 — Consider how well or poorly the value is represented in your current job. If you are unemployed, think of a past position. Again, rate it on a scale of 1 to 5 where 1 stands for "very poorly represented in my current/past job" and 5, for "extremely well represented in my current job". This is the test of the existence of the given value at work.

Work Value	Description	Score 1	Score 2
Aesthetics	It is important to you to conduct your work where beauty is important.		
Achievement	It is important to have challenging goals and to achieve them.		
Balance	It is important to have balance between your work and private life, so you have enough time for your family, hobbies and other activities.		
Being helpful	It is important to you to be helpful to others.		
Change	It is important to you to experience change.		
Competition	It is important for you to measure your performance against others.		
Contribution to society	It is important that your work contributes to society.		
Creativity	It is important to be able to express yourself creatively through your work.		
Cutting-edge knowledge	It is important to work in an environment that is involved in the latest developments.		
Excitement	It is important to express your passion through your work.		
Flexibility	It is important to have flexible working hours.		
Freedom	It is important for you to feel free to choose what you do and the way you do it.		

Work Value	Description	Score 1	Score 2
Fun	It is important to have fun at work. The working environment should be fun.		
Growth	It is important to feel that you can grow at work.		
Independence	It is important to be able to design your own activities without supervision.		
Innovation	It is important to work on innovative ideas and to come up with them yourself.		
Integrity	It is important to work for an organization that has high standards and enacts its values. It is important to work in a place that supports your values and beliefs.		
International	It is important to be exposed to an international environment, to travel internationally and to work with international colleagues.		
Leadership	It is important for you to lead others and to give direction to the organization.		
Learning	It is important to you to continuously learn new things at work.		
Money	It is important to you to earn a high salary.		
Physical fitness	It is important to be physically active at work.		

Work Value	Description	Score 1	Score 2
Power	It is important to have power over others, and to make key decisions.		
Professionalism	It is important to act professionally at work. It is important that your workplace supports professionalism and that it allows you to master your skills.		
Recognition	It is important that others recognize and value your work and that you have an important and prestigious job.		
Respect	It is important to feel that people have a high regard for who you are, irrespective of your race, sex and religious convictions.		
Responsibility	It is important to you to be able to fully accomplish the tasks that are assigned to you.		
Risk taking	It is important that your job requires you to take higher than average risks. It is important that your work requires you to make decisions with many unknowns.		
Security	It is important to have secure working conditions (a permanent contract).		

Work Value	Description	Score 1	Score 2
Social impact	It is important to do work in an organization that has a social impact. It is important that you have a direct social impact (through your own work).		
Stability	It is important to know what will happen each day. It is important to you to have thoroughly explained, organized and foreseen responsibilities.		
Status	It is important to be admired by, and to have influence over, others.		
Team work	It is important for you to work in an organization that thrives on common effort. It is important to work as part of a team.		
Variety	It is important to you to have variety in your work.		
Work alone	It is important to you to work independently.		

Step 2

Write down all the values that you scored highest (4/5).

Step 3

Write down your top 10, and then top 5 work values.

Step 4

For your top 5 values, write down stories from your work that support those values. So, in other words, can you come up with examples of situations that support the choice of these values?

Step 5

Check the second score (Score 2) for your top 5 values. How well are these values represented in your current job?

1. _____
2. _____
3. _____
4. _____
5. _____

» What does it tell you about your current career?

_____

_____

» What does it tell you about your future career?

_____

_____

Step 6

Write down the values you scored lowest (1/2).

» Are those values present in your career now?

_____

_____

Conclusions

After every chapter I will ask you to draw conclusions related to what you have discovered about yourself. This is a great way to reflect on what you have learned and discovered in a given chapter. The last chapter of this part of the book is "Putting the puzzle pieces together". By reflecting and reaching your conclusions after every chapter, you are doing great groundwork. It will make it so much easier to find out what your next career steps should be.

My top three core values are:

_____

_____

My top three work values are:

_____

_____

What have I learned about myself and my career in this chapter?

_____

_____

What ideas do I now have about the direction in which I want my career to grow?

_____

_____

Clients' Stories

Vera

"In everyday life, I kept myself busy to avoid confronting and listening to my inner self. But Dorota dared to force me to confront myself!"

Originally I'm a girl from the hotel business. I stayed in the business, working in different countries, for 10 years. I eventually changed to event management, again working in various countries. The last company I worked for was severely hit by the 2008 financial crisis and went bankrupt. After four months of unemployment, I found a job in the nuclear marketing department of a big engineering company.

This coincided with my ending an abusive relationship, and the new job was perfect for me at that point: nine to five, nobody knew me, no hassle, no stress — the perfect environment to heal and rebuild myself.

My original idea was to stay there for two and a half to three years and then move on, as this highly administrative environment didn't match my personality.

I bought a flat, and as I was solely responsible for the mortgage, I felt that I needed a secure, stable job. Two and a half years became seven years before I finally left the company.

In 2012, I started diving to conquer my fear of water. This step — and setting foot on Egyptian soil for the first time — profoundly changed something within me.

Yet it took another three years before I listened to my inner voice, which was telling me that the way my life was going wasn't making me happy. I knew all along that I didn't enjoy what I was doing, but I didn't know what I really wanted for myself or from life.

A very good friend who was unemployed for a long time went through the coaching process with Dorota, which helped her to land a job again. Though her needs were completely different to mine, I asked her if Dorota could also help people like me, who don't know what they want. She put us in touch.

Why did I consider the coaching process? I knew I was unhappy in my current job, but I also knew there was no point in changing companies or jobs. Within six months of starting a new job, I would be back to square one: restless and unhappy.

Of course my family and my friends all gave me good and wise counsel about what to do and how to do it. But somehow I knew that I would advance only if I got the point of view of an outsider, someone who did not know me or my situation, someone with a neutral take on the situation.

And so my journey started. First, Dorota and I had a Skype call (we live in different countries and have never met in person) to find out whether we would be able work together. Check!

In February 2015, we had our first coaching session, which included the "Timeline" exercise (page 63) and Maslow's "Pyramid of Needs" (page 36). Looking back on the "Timeline" exercise, it's amazing to see that I am now completely on track!

We met on Skype every two weeks or so. Dorota always gave me homework: review the previous session and do the exercises she sent.

You have no idea how much I hated these exercises, the homework and certain moments of our sessions!

Why? Because I had to confront myself. I had to turn my focus inwards, ask questions and be honest with myself. In everyday life, I kept myself busy to avoid confronting and listening to my inner self. And now Dorota had dared to force me to confront myself...

At more than one point, I just wanted to say, "Fuck it! Just do these stupid exercises yourself; I'm not going to do them! This is none of your business and I don't want to think about it!"

But what can I say? I care about money, and the fact that I had paid a substantial amount for this coaching kept me going in moments of loathing the work.

Slowly but surely a different kind of thinking emerged, and I started to see more clearly. I definitely knew what I DID NOT want any longer and had a better idea of what I DID want in life. But the question of how to make it happen was yet to be answered.

The mission statement I developed during the coaching was, "I play an active role in sustainable and effective protection of our oceans as well as aquatic life." My mantra? "I'm the firefighter of the oceans!"

In June that year I went on a special diving course to a secluded hotel in Egypt — a rather different hotel to what I had experienced previously. When I saw their slogan, "Welcome Home", my first thought was, "Yeah, right! Typical marketing blah blah!"

But by the second day I felt that there was something different about this hotel. This slogan really fitted and I felt completely at home.

Twice a week, the hotel organizes an evening for "solo travelers". All guests traveling alone are invited for a cocktail followed by dinner together.

As I have a big mouth and because I am a diver, I meet new people very easily so I didn't feel the need to be part of this evening. But, if you offer me a free cocktail, you win!

I happened to sit next to the personal assistant to the GM during dinner. She started to tell me her life story and that she had to go back to her home country at the end of the year for this and that reason.

As I mentioned, I have a big mouth and when combined with a few cocktails, things can sometimes get interesting!

Jokingly, I said, "Oh, don't worry about going back to your home country and leaving your GM without a PA! I've been in the hotel business, speak all the required languages, hate my job and am about to change my life. I'll take over your job!" She was incredulous. "Are you serious?" she asked. "Yes, sure!" was my response. She presented me to the GM, and after a two-minute chat across tables and chairs, he asked me to send him my CV when I got back home. He said they'd give me a call later that year.

Back in Europe, I continued my everyday life, continued my coaching with Dorota and continued to form ideas about what I would do in the future.

But there was a seed in the back of my mind, growing and teasing me. I talked to Dorota, my sister and my father about it. We all (including me) said, "Yeah, we'll see what happens in November!"

On the 16th of that month, I received the call. "Are you still interested? When can you start?"

My heart skipped a beat, and my first thought was, "Shoot, you and your big mouth! Are you going to go through with it or are you all talk?"

You can't imagine the rollercoaster of feelings I experienced in the first few seconds. Then the questions started. My own one was, "Yes, but should you leave your secure job (even though you hate it) for the unknown?" Then my father chimed in with, "Have you thought about the political situation in Egypt?" My sister, with index finger raised, said, "Don't forget, you're not getting any younger. Think about your pension", and the Belgian family's and Dorota's take was, "Of course you should go, you hate your job here and you'll never get another opportunity like that again. What do you have to lose?

Once I'd made my decision, everything happened very quickly. On 20 November, I signed the contract, on the 24th, I resigned from my job and in January 2016, I started my new job in Egypt as personal assistant to the GM of the most wonderful hotel, The Breakers, Soma Bay. Now I'm in my third year in Egypt and I haven't regretted this decision for a second!

Since that January, I have lived an enchanted life. My home and work is 10 meters from the Red Sea. I have a fulfilling job with great colleagues, in great surroundings. I can dive whenever I want to, and I have sun and blue sky all year round. Work doesn't feel like work anymore — it is pure pleasure.

The pace of my life is far slower than it was in Europe and I am really amazed at how easily I have adapted to it. I am completely balanced and at peace.

My mission statement and mantra haven't changed. During the coaching, I saw myself fighting actively in the field for one NGO or another. Working among active divers and kiters is a different platform, but the mission remains the same. The solo traveler meetings, which are now organized by me, are a great platform for informing interested guests about my beloved sharks and the need to protect the ocean.

I am convinced that things happen for a reason. If I hadn't been engaged in the coaching process, I would never have said something along the lines of, "Hey, I'll take over your job."

Thanks to the continuous coaching, I was open-minded and alert to opportunities. Even if my conscious mind had not reacted, my subconscious immediately saw the potential of this conversation, prompting me to speak out. Without the coaching, I would have stayed in my closet and said nothing.

When I was starting to write my story for Dorota's book, I leafed through my "Happiness Book" (a kind of diary I use occasionally to pencil in thoughts and that I used for my coaching and related homework). I stumbled on a note from October 2014. I'd written: "It's high time you changed your life. Get your bum moving and change something. I give you one year to prepare your new life. By Spring 2016, or, even better, December 2015, you will start this new life."

I hadn't seen or thought about this note in more than three years. But I had made the change anyway! I had stuck to my own timeline and started my new life in January 2016.

If you are also struggling with your life and career, go for coaching! It is worth the money as it will help you to gain clarity and know yourself better — if you find the right coach for you. (Coaching is becoming more and more of a trend and there are so many fakes out there so I was really lucky to find Dorota immediately.)

If you try to get through your struggle on your own or with the help of those close to you, you might not be able to get off your hamster wheel. It helps to have an outsider look at your patterns and your life because they look at you with a fresh, unbiased eye.

Chapter Six

How? Your talents

"Talent is cheaper than table salt.
What separates the talented individual
from the successful one is a lot of hard work."
Stephen King

The science behind talent

The birth of talent means the death of thousands of brain cell connections. In their book, *Now, discover your strengths,* Donald O. Clifton and Marcus Buckingham explain why and how it happens. When we are born, we have approximately 100 billion neurons (nerve cells) and until we reach our third year, each of these neurons creates 15,000 connections. Can you imagine how many connections there are in total? Trillions! A connection between two brain cells (neurons) is called a synapse. The synapses form circuits out of which our behavior is woven. Our behavior depends on the existence and strength of these connections.

So basically the synapses make our talents, and areas where there is a lack of synapses point to our weaknesses. Then an interesting thing happens; between the ages of three to 16 years, half of this network disappears and most of it cannot be restored. The connections that are not used are destroyed so that the others can become stronger.

Put simply, our talents use our strongest, and therefore fastest, connections in our brain. Our genetic material, mostly, but also our experience during our early years, decide which of these connections stay and which will be destroyed.

The process of growing up is focused on strengthening and increasing the speed of the connections. Why? In our daily life we have to make thousands of decisions. If these connections were not strong enough, we would not be able to make any decisions. Nature ensures that our strongest connections survive and are used.

Now the crucial question is: how can we strengthen our talents (brain connections)? It is done by practice, practice and more practice. When you use your talents, you strengthen the connections in your brain, which in turn allows you to excel at them. If, on the other hand, you are using your weaknesses, it is like trying to pump life into something that is dead or very, very weak. It will cost you lots of time and energy but, more importantly, you will most likely never reach the level of mastery.

So how can we rediscover our talents? Many people believe that talented people are those who can paint, sing or act. These, of course, are talents. However, we all possess different types of talents. The difficult thing is that our talents are so natural to us that we tend not to see them as talents. We believe that everyone can do the same thing. THIS IS NOT TRUE!

I do suggest that you take a test to discover your top five strengths. You can find it on www.gallupstrengthscenter.com and it is called *Top 5 CliftonStrengths*.

Warm-up exercise: Left hand, right hand

Whether you are thinking of changing your career, getting a new job or starting up your business, it is of utmost importance to understand what your talents are. Not using your talents means that you are employing weaknesses at work. This, as you will find out below, drains your energy and deprives you of self-confidence.

We will start with a warm-up exercise. On a piece of paper, write down your name and surname with the hand that you usually write with — your right hand if you are right-handed or your left hand if you are left-handed.

» How did you feel when you were writing?

_____

_____

Now do the same (write your name and surname) but with the other hand — your left hand if you are right-handed or your right hand if you are left-handed.

» Again, how did you feel when you were writing?

_____

_____

Most of my clients describe the first part as easy, done without thinking, effortless, while they describe the second part of the exercise as feeling strange, feeling like a child, frustrating, self-conscious, not in control etc.

This is exactly what happens to us when we use our talents or weaknesses. Now imagine that you were supposed to write with your other hand (the one you don't use for writing) all your life. Of course you would eventually learn to do it, but think of how much time and energy it would cost you. And what would happen to your skill of writing with the hand you do use for writing? It would deteriorate, as you would not be practicing. So in the end you would forget how to write with your "first" hand and become just average at writing with the other hand. This often happens with our talents. We focus so much on improving our weaknesses that we do not have time and/or energy left to master our talents and make them shine. What a waste!

Exercise: Discover your talents through your childhood

"Hide not your talents, they for use were made,
What's a sundial in the shade?"
Benjamin Franklin

The first exercise allows you to look back and reflect on your childhood. Our talents manifest themselves very early in our lives. It is then that our talent is still pure and unspoiled by the outside influence of schools, teachers etc.

If you do not remember what you excelled at as a child, ask your parents, grandparents or other relevant people for their feedback.

Please answer the questions below. Do it quickly and intuitively.

» What kept you busy as a child?

_____

» What were your favorite games as a child?

_____

» What in particular were you good at as a child?

_____

» During which activities were you happiest as a child?

_____

» What kind of child were you?

_____

» When growing up, what did people tell you that you had a talent for?

_____

_____

» Which of your activities were encouraged/discouraged by your parents?

_____

» Which of your talents that were present in your childhood are you still using now?

_____

Exercise: Feedback from people around you

"When I stand before God at the end of my life, I would hope that I would not have a single bit of talent left, and I could say, 'I used everything you gave me.'"
Erma Bombeck

Very often it is difficult for us to pinpoint what we are good at. This stems from the fact that we often believe that our talents are normal and that everyone else can do that too. This is why one of the best ways to find out what our talents are, is to ask people around us for their feedback.

Ask at least ten people around you to tell you what they see as your top five talents. Select a mix of friends, family, colleagues (peers/boss); that way you will get feedback on your talents in different areas of your life.

Once you receive the response from the people you have selected, take a moment to reflect on it by answering the following questions:

» What are the talents that others see in me? (List everything)

_____

» What talents do others see in me that I was not aware of?

_____

» Which of my talents do I neglect?

_____

_____

» Which of my talents make me feel proud of myself?

_____

_____

» Which of my talents make me happiest?

_____

_____

Exercise: Seven Stories

This is one my favorite exercises regarding talents. It comes from the famous book on careers, *What Color is Your Parachute?*[2], by Richard Bolles. You need to write a minimum of seven real-life stories in the manner explained below. Thanks to this exercise, you will be able to track down actions that you took that led you to your talents. The more stories you write, the more patterns in your behavior you will notice. And, then, as a result, your talents will become evident. As mentioned previously, our talents are so embedded in our DNA that it is very difficult to spot them as we think that most people behave in this way. We often think it is a not big deal. But it is!

Please write seven stories. Each story should have the following parts:

1. Description of your goal. What did you want to achieve?

_____

_____

2. Description of any obstacles you came across and needed to overcome to reach your goal (internal or external).

_____

_____

---

2   PERMISSION granted — see the Permissions page.

3. Description of what you did, step by step.

_____

_____

4. Description of the outcome/achievement.

_____

_____

You can use stories from both your professional and private life that are examples of when you achieved a positive outcome.

Once you have completed your seven stories, underline all the actions you took and think about which talents/skills helped you to accomplish your goal.

Questions to answer

» What are the talents that I used in the above-mentioned stories?

_____

_____

» Which patterns in my behavior do I notice?

_____

_____

» What conclusions can I reach, based on the stories above, related to my own talents or skills?

_____

_____

I will share a couple of stories from my clients, to show you the point of this exercise.

Magda's stories

Story #1 Finding work abroad; moving to the Netherlands

1. Describe your goal; what did you want to achieve?

After graduating from my business studies course in Poland, I wanted to move abroad and find a job that was related to my studies. I wanted to gain international work experience, meet people from all over the world, perfect my English, learn a new language, see new places, and get to know new cultures.

2. Describe any obstacles you came across (internal or external).
   » The number of job offers abroad was limited
   » I didn't know much about how to find a job abroad
   » I lacked self-confidence
   » I felt fearful of doing a job interview in a foreign language
   » I was fearful of my family's reaction. And I feared the unknown.

3. Describe what you did, step by step.
   ✓ The first step was to make a decision, "Yes, I want to move abroad." I became 100% sure of it, with no more doubts.
   ✓ Next, I looked at my options. Could I find a job abroad through my current employer? Could I find a recruitment company to help me to find a job abroad? I followed daily offers on a job board.
   ✓ When I saw an advertisement for a job in finance in Amsterdam, I reacted quickly; I sent the application the same day (later I found out that I was the first to apply).
   ✓ I was invited for an interview.
   ✓ I put a lot of time and effort into preparing for it.
   ✓ I was very nervous during the interview but my thorough preparation really helped and I got the job.
   ✓ I have to admit I had some doubts about the job offer, but I was determined to move abroad.
   ✓ The difficult part was informing my family that I was moving. They were worried about letting me go abroad alone. But I was completely sure of my decision. So I made all the arrangements and I left.

4. Describe the outcome/achievement.
   I realized my dream of moving abroad. And I learned that if I want something badly enough, I can do it.

Story #2 Learning to swim

1. Describe your goal; what did you want to achieve?
   At the age of 28, I finally wanted to learn to swim and to beat my fear of deep water.

2. Describe any obstacles you came across (internal or external).
   » I was frightened of deep water.
   » I believed that I was too old to learn to swim.
   » I believed that I was just never going to learn to swim and that it was unimportant to me.

3. Describe what you did, step by step.
   ✓ I registered for a swimming course. I attended the classes. I got up very early every day to train before I went to work. By 6 am, I was already in the swimming pool, which was completely empty at that hour. But after a year I could swim only with the help of a board. I stopped.
   ✓ Two years later, I started the whole process again. I found a small swimming pool with water that came up to my waist, near where I lived. I enrolled for the kids' swimming classes twice a week and bravely endured their looks and laughter. Finally I succeeded in swimming a meter all by myself. I was so happy!
   ✓ After some time I got my swimming diploma.

4. Describe the outcome/achievement.
   I learned to swim. I defeated my fear of deep water. I proved to myself that I could learn something new even if I am terrified of doing it.

Story #3 Finding volunteer work in Nepal

1. Describe your goal; what did you want to achieve?
   I was experiencing a tough time at work, and I felt I needed some time off. My dream was to do some volunteer work in Asia.

2. Describe any obstacles you came across (internal or external).
   » I had to make the time.
   » I had to find the right organization to volunteer for.
   » I lacked self-confidence.

3. Describe what you did, step by step.
   ✓ After a lot of searching on the Internet, I finally found an orphanage in Nepal that was looking for volunteers.
   ✓ I contacted them and offered my help. I sent them all the required documents, like my CV and motivation letter. They replied that they would be happy to have me there. The most difficult part was to actually quit my job. I didn't have any new job offers at that time. But I just did it. It felt like the right thing to do.
   ✓ I spent a couple of weeks volunteering in the orphanage and a couple more weeks traveling through Asia with a friend.

4. Describe the outcome/achievement.
   Once again, I proved to myself that if I really want something, I can get it. Also, I am not afraid to make tough decisions in order to realize my dreams and goals.

Story #4 Running a marathon

1. Describe your goal; what did you want to achieve?
   My new dream was to run a marathon.

2. Describe any obstacles you came across (internal or external).
    - » I had to learn to run in a group.
    - » I had to convince my body to make a huge effort despite the pain and the constant mental protests.

3. Describe what you did, step by step.
    - ✓ The first step was coming up with the idea of running a marathon. Immediately after the idea came to me, I started to doubt it. Why should I do it? Is it actually healthy to run such a long distance?
    - ✓ After some consideration, I finally decided that I did want to do it. I started with Internet research on how to prepare for a marathon.
    - ✓ I decided that I had the best chance of doing it if I trained with others. So I found a running club.
    - ✓ I trained twice a week. After five months of training, I ran my first marathon, and I reached the finish line in **4 hours and 22 minutes!**

4. Describe the outcome/achievement.
    I achieved my planned timing for the marathon without any injuries. I met some great people and found that running with a group is fun. And once again, I proved to myself that I can achieve whatever I want, once I set my mind to it.

Which talents did I use in the above-mentioned examples?
Patience
Determination
Competing against myself
Not giving up when things get rough
Great at research
Well prepared
Always looking for new challenges (physical and mental)

Hardworking
Decisive
Courageous
Consistent

Which behavior patterns do you notice?
- » When I want something, I take action. I make a plan but I don't rush into it, I give myself time to think.
- » I think a very important thing is that I actually stick to the plan.
- » When I really want something, I can overcome my feelings of insecurity.

What conclusions can you reach, based on the stories above, related to your talents?
I think the most important conclusion is that I can do so much more than I think I can. I often feel quite insecure about myself and my abilities, but once I look at what I have achieved — running a marathon, learning to swim as an adult, moving abroad and volunteering in Nepal — I know I can achieve anything once I put my mind to it and make a plan.

Yoli's stories

Story #1 Finding work in the non-profit sector

1. Describe your goal; what did you want to achieve?
   When I was working in consulting, I realized that part of me was not happy there, and I thought about working in the social sector, at an NGO. Since I was 14, I had dreamed of working for the UN and an NGO would give me the experience to head me in that direction.

2. Describe any obstacles you came across (internal or external).
   I had no experience, no network there, and my academic background was business.

3. Describe what you did, step by step.

    Part of me thinks it was mostly luck, being in the right place at the right time, as my boss helped me. Though, surely something about me had to motivate him to do so. He introduced me to two leads and also prepped me on what to say and what questions they might ask, like, "So you want to save the world?"

    Through those two leads I started networking, I prepared my CV, and prepared myself thoroughly for interviews. After a couple of interviews I got volunteer work at an NGO, and a potential interview at the United Nations in Mexico. After a month of volunteering, I was offered a job (with VERY little pay) at the NGO, and I took it. The UN came through at exactly the same time. I think I had a very good interview with the head of the agency and he decided to take a risk in appointing me to head a youth program, despite having no experience whatsoever in the field or NGO procedures.

4. Describe the outcome/achievement.

    It was a difficult first year, but I studied hard, learned fast and grew up fast. I managed to set up the basis of the program in Mexico and get some partners. We went on to achieve our goals for the first three years.

Story #2 Mexicans in Holland for Peace in Mexico

1. Describe your goal; what did you want to achieve?

    The situation in Mexico had become increasingly violent and out of control over the previous few years, due to the president's War on Drugs. After a particularly shocking murder, Mexicans gathered to march to say we had had enough. During the Dutch version of this march, I met other Mexicans who were equally concerned, had seen the call to meet in The Hague, and wanted to do something. After the initial march, we started a group that organizes activities to help Mexicans to be more aware of and sensitive to the problems back home, and that provides an opportunity to help.

2. Describe any obstacles you came across (internal or external).

   Those of us who made up the group were very different, sometimes with conflicting backgrounds. I felt that I played a big role in keeping it going and helping it grow.

3. Describe what you did, step by step.

   I did a lot of the coordination and strategic thinking, but all the blanks were filled in through team effort.

   I drew on a lot of skills that I had developed at my regular job at the NGO, such as communication, writing and event organizing skills.

   We created an online community of Mexicans for peace, which provides a constant stream of news and campaign suggestions for Mexicans here. We raised money for the peace movement in Mexico, and celebrated two Mexican holidays in remembrance of the struggle, which is ongoing.

4. Describe the outcome/achievement.

   It has been very tough to keep it up, as it is not a "pretty" topic to work on. As a result of working for this cause, we are much more aware of the deaths, which are often particularly gruesome. On the other hand, it is rewarding to see that it matters to some people, and to feel that, at the very least, we are increasing awareness.

   For something that's voluntary, not always easy, and done by a handful of people in our free time, I think we have achieved a lot.

Which talents have I used in the above-mentioned examples?

   Social consciousness
   Persuasiveness
   Communication skills
   Hardworking capability
   Organizing skills
   Writing skills

Motivating the team
Volunteering
Determination
Perseverance
Getting things done

Which behavior patterns do you notice? What conclusions can you reach, based on the stories above, related to your talents?

» I care a lot about social causes and I am prepared to work very hard for them.

» I think my main strengths lie in perseverance and getting things done.

Your talent map

"According to this law [the law of Dharma], you have a unique talent and a unique way of expressing it. There is something that you can do better than anyone else in the whole world — and for every unique talent and unique expression of that talent, there are also unique needs. When these needs are matched with the creative expression of your talent, that is the spark that creates affluence. Expressing your talents to fulfill needs creates unlimited wealth and abundance."
Deepak Chopra

The drawing below allows you to discover your talents based on the different ways you manifest them. For example, a mental talent could be the ability to solve complex problems, a talent related to the heart could be empathy, a talent related to your senses could be a good ear for music or noticing details others miss.

Once you have filled in your talent map, consider which of your talents you use most and which, least.

Talents related to
my mind:

Talents related to
my senses (ears,
eyes, etc.):

Talents related to
my heart:

Talents related to
my intuition &
creativity:

Talents related to
my hands:

Talents related to my
body (i.e. sports):

Any other talent:

My Talent Map

Conclusions

After every chapter, I want you to reflect on what you have discovered about yourself. The last chapter of this part of the book is "Putting the puzzle pieces together". By reflecting and reaching some conclusions after every chapter, you are doing the groundwork for this chapter. It will make it so much easier to find out what your next career steps should be.

My top five talents are:

_____

_____

The talents that make me most happy are:

_____

_____

What have I learned about myself and my career in this chapter?

_____

_____

What ideas do I have at this point about the direction in which I want my career to grow?

_____

_____

Clients' Stories

Marieke

"People who know you put you in a certain box and direct you towards the kinds of opportunities fitting that box. If you want to move out of the box, they will never really be able to help you."

I have a lot of big company names on my CV and had a great education. With that package, I should have been at the level of director, but I had not reached that when I decided to embark on coaching. One of the reasons is that I was following my husband from one country to another. Each time, I found a job that was similar to my previous one, but in a different industry. Because of the parallel moves, I did not progress — neither upwards, nor in the direction I really wanted. The job functions themselves were good, but the industries I worked in did not really suit me; they did not make me proud. I wanted to feel better about myself. You could call it a midlife crisis.

The reason I chose to study civil engineering in the first place was because I wanted to do something good — to bring water to Third World countries. But somehow I never got to do anything substantial, either socially or environmentally. Whenever we moved to another country, I tried again, but when you switch countries it is very difficult to switch the direction of your career at the same time. It left me with a career with little real purpose, below the level I should have attained.

I came to Dorota with a two-fold challenge. One was how to get into a managerial position and the other, how to do so in an industry or company that was contributing something positive to the world.

Before I left my previous company, I asked the people I was leading, "If I wanted to do something good in the next step in my career, what could you see me doing?" A lot of people suggested that I start coaching, as this is what I had been to them: their leader and their coach. Although I liked this option, I felt my next step needed to be bigger, more significant. I wanted to have a positive impact on more than one person. I am sure it is great to help even one person and that it leaves you satisfied but I felt I could do more.

I decided to find myself a career coach because I had worked with some previously, and they had helped me to take a couple of steps forward. If you are motivated to change, you can think of options yourself, but real change is difficult to push through. I think you can go forward with much more focus if somebody is at your side to help you. Theoretically your partner could do that, but he or she sees you in a certain way, does not really want to change you, and is simply too emotionally attached to be objective. People who know you (like your partner, parents, friends) put you in a certain box and direct you towards opportunities fitting that box. If you want to move out of the box, they will never really be able to help you.

Instead, you need somebody who will ask you neutral questions that will help your thinking process, and give you a kick in the butt every once in a while. An objective person will help keep you motivated towards that desired change, keep your eye on the light at the end of the tunnel, and help you take the appropriate steps.

A coach fulfills that role. With his or her help, you avoid falling into the trap of continuing with the same type of job you've always had, simply because it doesn't require the effort of change.

My goal was concrete: to find one or two quite specific career tracks for the next five to ten years and beyond; to compile compelling wording in my LinkedIn profile that would generate respect and career leads; to identify one or two potential specific, realistic job positions with target companies; to adapt my CV for each, and, finally, to make contact with suitable companies.

During the initial sessions with Dorota, we looked at my values and passions — the things that made me tick. This slowly helped me to create a mission statement: "To achieve the unimaginable by linking, motivating and leading groups and organizations." I also discovered that I am particularly motivated and inspired by the battle against climate change.

My ideal job would contain the elements that had given me professional satisfaction throughout my career. I'd need to be involved in developing people, and to be a "linchpin" dealing with stakeholders for an international company with a product I truly believed in. Also, the job would need to provide me with sufficient remuneration. It would do all that, but more — it would have a purpose, it would make a contribution to people and planet.

Further exploration helped me to understand what it was in each of these tracks that attracted me and to what degree that was offset by the less attractive aspects of each. Three main threads started to appear: being an entrepreneur, leading a smaller organization with a good cause, and working in an NGO.

I explored the NGO path intensively: networking in this new terrain allowed me to talk to many people about how to make a career transition into that field. The one issue that arose was whether it really was a good fit for me.

At the same time, I looked at the entrepreneurial track, specifically green startups. I found most of my new contacts on LinkedIn, some of them through Dorota. It surprised me how almost everyone was willing to spend time with me brainstorming about my career: most people love to help with thinking, as long as they are not asked directly for a job.

During all this networking, I made one important decision: to really change my career, for the better this time.

Through a new acquaintance I met at a birthday party, I was fast-tracked for a position as business development director at an innovative startup in the energy sector. I really liked the company for its people, working culture and innovation, but the match wasn't perfect: the company's product wasn't as green or socially focused as I would have liked. The position was entirely focused on the product, and very little on people management; I would not even have my own team. Even though I went on to the last round and would almost certainly have landed the job, I decided that the product focus was not what I wanted so I stepped out of the process. It was a difficult decision to take, but I'm glad I stuck to my goals.

While several other leads didn't work out for different reasons, three seemed particularly positive. A friend had founded a startup in renewable energy, so I was able to do some voluntary work in business development, which was a great opportunity to experience the early stages of a startup, in the exact area of my interest, and build credibility in that field at the same time. I also came across an advertisement for a job at a sustainability consultancy firm. The company was looking to expand to the Netherlands and needed a country director. I knew I had a great chance of getting the job as I had previous experience in setting up companies and also in setting up a consultancy network. I decided to give it my all: this was the best match between my aspirations and experience. The third opportunity, which I cherished, was teaching business writing classes at a leading university. Even though I did not want to teach or coach full-time, this was a perfect add-on to my career!

In getting to this point, the coaching process played a pivotal role. It is crucial to understand what drives you and makes you thrive. Dorota gave me various exercises that, in combination, were very powerful. The exercises enable you to see what is really important to you. I had done several of them in some form or another in previous coaching sessions, but I had never realized the extent to which certain things bothered me. Connecting the dots was really important. For example, I needed to understand why I didn't want to become a coach or consultant, or why the NGO world was not the best fit for me. Digging deeper with Dorota's help did the trick.

The "Values" (page 86) exercise provided the insight that I needed to look for opportunities that would marry my four important values: family, money, respect and meaningful work. Balancing work and family time had ruled my career to that point, but money, title and meaningful work values had become increasingly important. If I didn't pay enough attention to the last two values now, halfway through my career, it would become more and more difficult for me to attain real career satisfaction.

After two to three months of working with Dorota, I gained one of my biggest insights: that I like and need very difficult challenges. I used this element during job interviews, as I noticed that interviewers love to hear of my determination to succeed in difficult situations.

My last job gave me another important insight, which was reinforced while working with Dorota: that you are valuable as you are — you don't have to be anyone else. When I am myself, I am at my strongest. If I am true to myself, with all my shortcomings, my passions, values and talents, I can succeed. Better yet, this increases the respect I get from others, which is very important to me.

Coaching crystallized lessons that were lingering in the background. It helped me to understand what I want, to "sell" myself better, and to put myself out there. If I hadn't been engaged in the coaching process, the urgency to earn money would have come first rather than the pursuit of real change in my career. Thanks to coaching I really stuck to what I wanted.

Making a change can take so long that you start feeling guilty about not having a job and not earning money. I wanted to be able to tell my friends that after all those months I had landed the job I had aimed for, otherwise I would have felt that I'd lost face.

I am really proud that I stuck to my mission and got a job at the right level in the type of organization I was aiming for. I chose for "green" and I really found my spot. I also have the flexibility to continue being a guest lecturer, which enriches me, as I really love to teach.

Making the change wasn't easy. I contacted about 10 people a week, and some weeks no one replied. I had many amazing meetings with people who provided me with valuable advice and insights, but some were less valuable, which was disappointing. In those moments, I questioned whether I could really make the transition.

And when I decided not to go for the first job offer, I didn't have an alternative. I felt like I was sliding down the hill and had to push myself up again. In those difficult times the coaching sessions helped a lot, particularly in regaining energy.

At this point, I am a couple of months into my new challenge. I am thoroughly enjoying learning about new topics like sustainability and acquiring new skills like sales and general management. I was afraid of selling; it takes me out of my comfort zone, but because I believe in the services of the company, it is, as Dorota says, selling from the heart. Learning new things is no effort as I am passionate about this work.

I feel like a fish in water! My new company is unpretentious, small and dynamic, and very open to new ideas, which means that I feel I can really add value. I feel respected. Because the mother company is in Belgium, it also has the international aspect I like so much. In short, it's a fantastic match!

Stepping up in my career has, however, increased the strain on my family life. Through coaching, I realized that I would not be able to overcome the value conflict between family and work. There is no way you can marry work and family perfectly. This remains painful.

For anyone else who is struggling career-wise, my advice is to talk! Ideally, talk to a coach regularly, or, if you don't have one, talk to people outside your direct circle of friends. It is extremely rewarding and stimulating to talk to people from different sectors, who have different perspectives, insights and advice. Talking helps shape and refine your thoughts; it helps you to find out what is really important to you. You'll be surprised to find out how many people actually want to help you. Even strangers. No, especially strangers!

A lot of people get stuck in their careers by following the highway — the easiest route — of convenience or sometimes necessity. You feel you cannot get out of the box: your environment, recruiters and headhunters try to force you to stay on the highway. Taking the little path into the bushes instead is daring and scary. It takes energy and courage, and you might not move as fast as on the highway. But the rewards at the end of that path are great. If you imagine yourself at 70, looking back on your life, what would you be most proud of?

It is also important to realize that you still have a long career in front of you. Most people hit a career crisis at around 40. You're not even halfway through your career! You still have plenty of time to completely change your career, difficult as it might seem. It is very depressing to think that you will be stuck doing something you do not want to be doing for the next 25 years or so. Even if a career change takes you a year, what is that year in comparison to the 25 following it?

There will be setbacks: for every two steps forward, you'll take one step backward. Real change takes time. Someone I met during a networking event told me that, on average, when you are around 40 it takes six months to get a new job. And if you also want to change your career, you need at least double that time. The more parameters you change, the longer it will take. Do not get discouraged.

It's a good idea to build a mechanism for dealing with setbacks so that you don't fall into depression. Having a coach can be a part of this. Regular talks with your coach will help you to keep your energy up. But other things can help too, like setting one objective a day or establishing a new rhythm by doing some type of exercise. And, if you apply for jobs, always make sure there are three applications in the pipeline. If one opportunity falls away, you are still left with hope for the other two.

Only you can drive the change; no one will do it for you. So allow yourself a time frame to figure out what it is that makes you happy and how you can get to your sweet spot. You will be forever grateful.

Chapter Seven

Why? Your life mission

"The mystery of human existence lies not in just staying alive, but in finding something to live for."
Fyodor Dostoyevsky, The Brothers Karamazov

My life purpose story

For many years, I thought I had found my life mission. After leaving my career in the corporate world to become a coach, I helped my clients to realize their own professional dreams and goals. I was working with people from all over the world, from very different professions. I felt so privileged to be their confidant, to help them when they struggled, to cheer them up when they doubted. And I am eternally grateful to the universe and myself for choosing this career path. But in 2017, I realized that I had yet another purpose to fulfill.

It happened during a Spirit Business Event. The main guest at the event was the amazing Gabrielle Bernstein, an American coach and spiritual guide, best known for her books, *Judgment Detox: Release the Beliefs that Hold You Back* and *The Universe Has Your Back*. To be honest, I must admit that I have a bit of a conflicted relationship with spirituality, as I've mentioned before.

However, during one of the Kundalini meditations guided by Gabby, I had a vision, which I shared with you in the Chapter One in the first part of this book — the vision of heavily pregnant mothers, wearing white turbans. I almost never cry, but the tears started to run down my face. I realized what my deeper life mission and purpose was: to save mothers from dying in childbirth. I realized that this was the meaning I wanted to give my near-death experience during my own delivery. One of my Mexican peer coaching friends told me, "Dorota, people who almost died are the souls who were sent back to earth to do something good." No child should be deprived of having its mama. Due to my personal experience, this mission touches me deeply.

I have decided that the profits from this book will go to support Zubaida Bai's company, ayzh.com, which designs healthcare products for women and girls living in resource-poor areas. Her most notable product is JANMA, a Clean Birth Kit in a Purse. Janma kits provide the sanitary tools and instructions to help women in resource poor areas survive their deliveries without infection. I have also decided to "come out of the closet" and start openly sharing my experience of childbirth. The more I talk, the more heads are thinking with me, and the clearer the way of fulfilling my purpose becomes. The doors start opening.

The intuitive way of discovering your life mission

Back to you now! One of the great ways to realize what your life mission is, is to look at your own life stories and experiences. The experiences may be painful, but not necessarily so.

> » What pain do you carry that you want to transform into a great cause?

_____

_____

> » Which life experience has marked you, and keeps resurfacing?

_____

_____

In my case, my delivery story kept coming back to me, but I was not open to listening to it. When I saw the vision during the meditation, I felt I could no longer deny it.

This is why I have designed a guided visualization for you. I believe that matters such as life mission and purpose are locked in our subconscious and the way to reveal them is by tapping into your intuitive mind, the right side of your brain. If, like me, you lean to the more rational, take my word for it and trust me. It might not come to you the first time, so please do not feel disappointed. It will come eventually, one way or another. Just be mindful and pay attention. Listen!

I have included the text of this visualization in the book, so you can ask a friend to read it to you. I have also recorded it and put on my website (www.dosocoaching.com/careerjump), so you can download it and listen to it when you are alone. The visualization on my website is accompanied by beautiful and powerful music, so I sincerely recommend listening to it. The important thing is that you do it, whatever the way.

Visualization

Please sit comfortably.
Put both your feet on the floor.
Allow your hands to rest gently on your lap.
Slowly close your eyes.

Take a deep breath.
Breathe in and out deeply a couple of times.
Relax your muscles.

Feel that you are safe.

Now, focus on yourself.
Focus on your dreams.

Give yourself permission to dream.
Give yourself permission to dream big.

Now take a moment and picture yourself living a happy and meaningful life.

Where are you?
What are the surroundings?
What are the colors and smells of this place?

What are you doing?
Who is with you?

How do you feel?

Free?
Empowered?
Purposeful?
Successful?
Happy?
Ready to achieve your dreams?

Now, when you are ready, take your time to come back to the present moment and to this location.

Feel the floor under your feet.
Feel the chair against your back.
Gently move your hands and feet.
You can stretch.
Take a deep breath.
Open your eyes.

Welcome back.

Now write down everything you have seen and experienced during this visualization.

The rational way

"It is not that we have so little time but that we lose so much...
The life we receive is not short but we make it so; we are
not ill provided but use what we have wastefully."
Seneca, On the Shortness of Life

In Chapter One, I described Maslow's hierarchy of needs and the fact that the ultimate step, the final needs reflected in the pyramid, are the needs of self-actualization, contribution and spirituality. When we look at it from the perspective of our career, we can say that this corresponds with the career that gives us the possibility not only to contribute to the happiness in our own lives but to the happiness of others. A meaning. Something that we care about. Something that will positively impact the lives of others. Something that is bigger than us. Something that answers the question WHY?

This is why even a well-paid career in a corporation stops being sufficient at a certain point (unless, of course, the mission of the corporation you are working for is in line with your own life mission). Many of my clients are then confronted with the feeling of guilt. If they compare themselves to friends or family members who have lower paid jobs, they start to feel bad about their own needs. They feel that they cannot want more for themselves if those close to them struggle with the basics. But this is a natural process when we look at it from the perspective of our needs. It is helpful if you realize that by staying unhappy and unfulfilled, you are not helping anyone.

Many of my female clients who have recently become mothers no longer feel fulfilled by their career. Often ambitious women who had great corporate careers feel that their job needs to be meaningful in order to compensate for the time that they are not at home with their children. But they also want to make the world a better place for them.

We all have a purpose. Our main purpose is to give the world the gift or talent that we were born with. When we contribute that to others, we start feeling that our life has meaning.

A lot of my clients are afraid to articulate their life mission. And when they do, they often feel uncomfortable about it initially, not realizing that this purpose and mission have long lain dormant, waiting to be discovered. When we become aware of our purpose, we come to life. We feel connected and purposeful. We have found our compass.

But how do you discover your mission and where and how you want to contribute? You need to look deep, deep into the core of your being and start by asking yourself this question:

What would I be doing in my life and career if money/diplomas were not an issue?

Important points to remember about your life mission:
- ✓ It does not need to be huge — just bigger than you
- ✓ Big enough to keep you motivated
- ✓ Within your control
- ✓ Close to your heart
- ✓ Positively formulated
- ✓ Has a positive impact on you
- ✓ Has a positive impact on others
- ✓ Is based on your talents

Here is a list of further questions that can help you to formulate your life mission / life purpose.

Exercise: My life mission

Step 1

Please answer the following questions.

1. What are your core values?

_____

_____

2. What would happen in your life, if you lived it fully honoring your values?

_____

_____

3. What are your natural talents?

_____

_____

4. When are you in the FLOW state (you are deeply focused on an activity and you completely lose a track of time)?

_____

_____

5. What are your talents that make you feel most fulfilled?

_____

_____

6. What are your talents that make you feel most proud?

_____

_____

7. What makes you unique?

_____

_____

8. What activities give you energy and make you feel confident about yourself?

_____

_____

9. What are your favorite activities to do privately and professionally?

    _____

    _____

10. If you knew you could not fail and money were not an issue, what would you be doing in your professional and private life?

    _____

    _____

11. What would give you a feeling of highest joy and fulfillment in your career?

    _____

    _____

12. What are you passionate about?

    _____

    _____

13. If someone Googled your name in five years' time, what would you like them to find/read about you?

    _____

    _____

14. If you could be a hero, who would you be and why?

    _____

    _____

15. Imagine you have one year to live from now on, what would you do?

    _____

    _____

16. What is the legacy you want to leave when you are gone?

    _____

    _____

17. What are the world's problems you care about?

    _____

    _____

18. What are the causes (organizations, movements) that are close to your heart?

_____

_____

19. What are the most difficult moments, experiences in your life that you could share with / teach others to their benefit?

_____

_____

20. Who would you like to inspire?

_____

_____

21. Imagine you are standing on a stage and there is a big crowd in front of you. What do you want to tell them that could positively impact their life?

_____

_____

22. If you could take over one talent from anyone in the world, what would that be, from whom and why?

Person 1 _____

Person 2 _____

Person 3 _____

Person 4 _____

Person 5 _____

23. If you could take three things to an uninhabited island (next to the practical things like food, drinks, clothing etc.) what would that be?

_____

_____

24. What are you most grateful for in your life?

_____

_____

25. When do you feel you your life has a higher purpose?

_____

_____

Step 2

Create your life mission statement

To create your mission statement, you need to identify four main elements: who do you want to contribute to which problem do you want to help solving + which top talents you want to use doing that (your unique combination of talents) + what is the outcome of your contribution (impact).

Please answer the following questions.

1. Have a look at your answers above and write down everyone and everything you want to contribute to.

_____

_____

2. What is the problem that you want to help solve?

_____

_____

3. Have a look at your answers above and also in Chapter Six and list all your talents, then distill the unique combination of your top (three) talents.

_____

_____

4. What is the outcome of your help? What is the impact you want to create?

_____

_____

5. Before writing your mission statement, take a big piece of paper and brainstorm it (based on the input from above). Then start writing it down, keep on rewriting until you feel deeply connected with your mission statement. It can take many rewrites to have it done, even 100. Do not stop until you feel the goose bumps. Remember, this is YOUR mission statement, so it can be as staid or quirky, daring or conservative, ordinary or extraordinary as YOU like.

MY MISSION STATEMENT IS:

_____

_____

_____

Isabella's mission statement

Below you can see the real-life example of the above exercise filled in by one of my clients.

Step 1
Please answer the following questions. Do this quickly, intuitively, and without overthinking.

1. What are your core values?
    family
    freedom
    respect
    care
    fun
    intelligence

2. What would happen in your life if you lived it fully honoring your values?
    I'd enjoy it to the full for half the week and be buried in the trenches for the other half week.

3. What are your natural talents?

    Conceptual thinking, extensive social networking, building alignments, writing, solving complex issues, idea generation, inspiring people (seeing more in people)

4. When are you in the FLOW state (so deeply focused on an activity that you completely lose track of time)?

    Creating a solution to a complex problem I have studied sufficiently

    Advising people one-on-one

    Taking photographs

    Writing

5. Which of your talents make you feel most fulfilled?

    Inspiring people to solve their own problems, seeing the problems solved and their personal growth in the process

    Implementing development or creating a piece of art

6. Which of your talents make you most proud?

    Analytical and conceptual problem solving

7. What makes you unique?

    My wide professional experience, my views and my extensive network

8. What activities give you energy and make you feel confident about yourself?

    A big project presentation, a photo project printed, written feedback

9. What are your favorite activities, privately and professionally?

    Meetings

    Brainstorming

    Reading

Quantitative tasks
Learning a new concept or discipline in a meeting / at an event

10. If you knew you could not fail and money were not an issue, what would you be doing in your professional and private life?
Writing a book
Writing magazine articles
Photography and movie making

11. What would give you the feeling of highest joy and fulfillment in your career?
Recognition through being published, an award

12. What are you passionate about?
Business, global topics, politics, writing, photography, film making

13. If someone Googled your name in five years' time, what would you like them to find/read about you?
A book I published
An award I received
Serving on the board of a public or humanitarian institution or as a member of a political party

14. If you could be a hero, who would you be and why?
Because he is my daugher's hero, and I do relate to him — organizing a team to save others, good morale, strong and brave.

15. Imagine you have one year to live from now. What would you do?
Write a book, coach and advise people

16. What is the legacy you want to leave when you are gone?
How people can overcome their problems, limitations, or health issues

17. Which of the world's problems do you care most about?
Inclusive growth
Healthcare
Mental and physical health
Political conflicts, terrorism

18. What are the causes (organizations, movements) that are close to your heart?
Doctors Without Borders, Bill & Melinda Gates Foundation, UN Millennium Development Goals, NATO

19. What are the most difficult moments or experiences in your life that you could share with / teach others to their benefit?
International cross-cultural career
Motherhood

20. Who would you like to inspire?
Leaders

21. Imagine you are standing on a stage and there is a big crowd in front of you. What do you want to tell them that could positively impact their life?
We have all the resources in the world to solve its complex problems. Sit in the trenches temporarily — you have the way out within yourself.

22. If you could take one talent from anyone in the world, what would that be, from whom and why?
Sheryl Sandberg or Richard Branson — business leadership in the international community while being yourself, and having fun; Indra Nooyi — leading the international cross-cultural community on the global financial and political scene; Zaha Hadid — creating for life, being yourself, having tangible creations and earning money and recognition for those internationally; Paulo Coelho — writing.

23. If you could take three things (besides practical items like food, drinks, clothing) to an uninhabited island, what would they be?
A book, a pen and a white piece of paper

24. What are you most grateful for?
My daughter, my husband and my family
International possibilities and freedom
Interesting life experiences

25. When do you feel your life has a higher purpose?
When I truly help an individual and see their eyes light up

Step 2

Create your life mission statement

To create your mission statement, you need to identify four main elements: who you want to contribute to + which problem you want to help solve + which top talents you want to use doing that (your unique combination of talents) + the outcome of your contribution (impact).

1. Have a look at your answers above and write down everyone and everything you want to contribute to.
Communities
Countries

2. What is the problem that you want to help to solve?
Inclusive growth
Innovative healthcare, or one of the global crises like terrorism

3. Have a look at your answers above and list all your talents, then distill the unique combination of your top (three) talents.
Complex analysis, conceptual thinking and driving for results

4. What is the outcome of your help? What is the impact you want to create?

   Change the system, specifically the healthcare, economic and business systems

5. Before writing your mission statement, take a big piece of paper and brainstorm it (based on the input from above). Then start writing it down and keep on rewriting until you feel deeply connected with your mission statement. It can take many rewrites to have it done — even 100. Do not stop until you feel the goose bumps. Remember, this is YOUR mission statement, so it can be as staid or quirky, daring or conservative, ordinary or extraordinary as YOU like.

MY MISSION STATEMENT IS:

I would like to change the economic system to ensure inclusive growth and to provide services and benefits, like health care, to all. The approach would be innovative, releasing a lot of wasted resources and fueling a sustainable model.

Conclusions

By now you already know the drill. So now please take time to reflect on this chapter and form some conclusions about what you have learned about yourself.

My life mission is:

_____

_____

What does this life mission mean for my career? What changes do I need to make in my career in order to fully embrace my life mission?

_____

_____

What have I learned about myself and my career in this chapter?

_____

_____

What ideas do I now have about the direction in which I want my career to grow?

_____

_____

Have I started to see a pattern?

_____

_____

Clients' Stories

N.S.

"At my core, I am a doer. My struggle arose from the fact that I could not do anything to solve my problem, because I had not identified it and felt stuck. Once I knew the solution, it was time for action."

I have been a corporate slave for a big part of my career. However, I believe I have been fortunate in that my jobs have been very fulfilling, and I have made a good career for myself in the corporate world. Over the past few years, though, I felt a pronounced lack of a creative outlet. I come from a very creative family. My grandfather was dressmaker to the Bollywood stars of the '50s and '60s and my mum is incredibly creative too. She made my clothes until I was well into my teens and I can tell you that I was the best-dressed girl at school for a long time. And now, my daughter has the most beautiful, unique dresses, thanks to her. My father was a very successful businessman, so you could say that business and creativity are in my genes.

I chose a different path — to be a fiercely independent, successful career woman in a predominantly male industry. I enjoyed the perks that came with it, but you can only run from your DNA for so long. I had a desperate itch to do something creative in fashion, so I took a break from corporate life and started working on my own company. My daughter was born at this time too. I was bootstrapping my company while we had a new human being to take care of! I needed to figure out how to finance my new life. To be honest, I missed the perks that came with the corporate environment, so I looked for another job. A full-time job + baby + company = bad idea. It was too much to handle so I closed my company.

I did not know it then, but that was the worst decision I have ever made. From that moment, I was LOST! I was confused and did not know my purpose. I called it my professional midlife crisis. I enjoyed my job, the employer culture, not so much. I tried looking for another job — but none of them inspired me. I was down in the dumps, so I did what most people do: I turned to family and friends for help. I have an incredibly supportive husband and friends who were there for me whenever I needed them. Seeing you suffer is difficult for your family and friends. Because they are so invested in you, I found that it is challenging for them to give objective advice that isn't confused by love and affection. Emotions have no logic; I needed someone to remove the emotion from what I was going through and help clear the clouds. For the first time in my life, I decided to ask for help from a professional.

I contacted a few coaching companies who worked with expats. Dorota was one of them. When I spoke to her, I felt a connection. I realized that I wanted someone to just listen to me, to let me describe what I was going through and only then to guide me through the process of figuring out my path. This process is difficult to follow with family and friends because they jump in too quickly to try to solve the problem. I should know; I do it all the time! I explained this to Dorota and she understood. She listened patiently while I ranted. I apologize for boring you so much, Dorota!

My objective for taking up coaching was simple: to figure out the cause of my confusion. I had never been as confused before and this was not making me happy. I am not into self-help books or inspirational quotes. The decision to get a career coach was a bit of a gamble as I was not sure if any of this "hocus-pocus" worked. I did not know what to expect. But I needed to do something, and I am glad I did.

After my initial session with Dorota, I wrote my first article on Medium, an online publishing platform. I used to enjoy writing. I like to tell stories. I had a blog when blogging was in its infancy. When my father passed away almost nine years ago, I stopped writing. I tried, but I just could not write any longer. This was the first time I had written in nine years! Dorota described it as "peeling the onion". I felt such relief. It was also the first sign that coaching was working for me. But while writing was the first breakthrough, clearing the clouds was still a bit further away.

As I started working through the exercises on talents, values, passions and so on, one realization that dawned on me was the importance specific values such as creativity, fun, community and business have for me. I knew these were important, but I did not realize just how significant they were. The exercises also made the reasons for my struggle very clear.

I particularly enjoyed the exercise on talents (page 104). It entailed asking my friends and family to tell me what they liked about me. We do not tend to compliment one another, so it was fun to hear them say nice things. The good news was that there were no surprises. They all confirmed my talents.

Then we came to the "Parent-Adult-Child model" (Chapter Thirteen). We did this exercise as a way of addressing something I was facing at work, but this is where I had my biggest breakthrough. As I stood looking at the piece of paper with "ADULT" written on it, I said out loud, "There is nothing I can do professionally that will make me as happy and fulfilled as running my own business in fashion." I had seen the light — much like Buddha! The clouds started to clear. I had read about this sort of revelation in the past and thought, "How can this be a breakthrough? There isn't any logic to it." I now know what that struggle feels like, as well as what it feels like to come out of it. It is so simple but admitting something to yourself out loud is probably the most difficult thing to do. From then on, I felt happy and contented.

When we worked on the "Life Mission" exercise (page 131), I told Dorota that my mission felt too lofty. It still does. She says it should be. It scares me put down my mission in words — out in the open. But here goes: "My Life Mission is to help communities living on aid become self-reliant through my business." I am still figuring out how to go about achieving this lofty goal.

The recently formulated mission for my company TalesonSilk is: "to create a platform to showcase tribal artists by collaborating together with them to create contemporary motifs. These artists are often simple people living in remote villages of India and dedicated to their art form. Some of them have achieved some recognition in that their paintings are being sold by the likes of Saatchi Art, however, these forms are still not well known in the global consciousness and my hope is that TalesonSilk will be a way to elevate their global standing."

Once my purpose was clarified, then came the fun part: figuring out what to do. My husband was very involved in my next steps. Dorota was sometimes surprised at how quickly I take action. She often said, "If all my clients were like you, I would be out of a job." The thing is, at my core, I am a doer. My struggle arose from the fact that I could not do anything to solve my problem, because I had not identified it and felt stuck. Once I knew the solution, it was time for action.

I set myself a goal and made a financial plan. I decided to work part-time and to try to scale my company until it generated a stable income. So far, I am happy to tell you that I am sticking to my plan. Hopefully it will come to fruition.

The exercises have also been useful in my current job. I sometimes use the "Parent-Adult-Child model" (Chapter Thirteen) with my team members. One of them, who is quite reserved, recently opened up to me and I do think it was as a result of this approach.

I also make sure I think about my shadow talents in a positive light — something I did not do before. As you can see, I have gained a lot from these sessions.

I do not wish the internal conflict that I went through on anyone. Let me also say that I fully recognize that I live a charmed life and that the issues I have described are most definitely luxury problems. But even the privileged go through tough times and if you do, I recommend seeking professional help. Take a leap of faith and go through this process. You might be surprised at what you learn about yourself.

Chapter Eight

What? Your passions

"Man is only great when he acts from passion."
Benjamin Disraeli

How to discover your passion?

Imagine that you wake up every day with a feeling of excitement.
Excited about what the new day will bring.

Excited because you know that what you do is what you love.

Excited because you know that your work is what you were born to do.

Excited because you feel that what you do matters.

Excited because what you do is an expression of your gifts.

What would your life look like if you had found your passion and were able to make your career out of it?

Okay, so far so good. But what if you, like myself in the past and like many of my clients, do not know what your passion is? Or even worse, what if you are afraid that you do not have any passions? What to do then? And why don't we know it (anymore)?

When did we stop dreaming?

I notice that many of my clients know what they are passionate about but they are either afraid to admit what it is or do not take it seriously themselves. Why? Mostly because they are afraid of what others will think of it.

Passion is a matter of the heart, not of the head. So it is often difficult to find it by only thinking about it. We can find it by feeling and doing it. The problem is that often our rationality takes over at an early age.

Good intentions, negative impact

Do you remember who you wanted to become when you grew up? And do you remember the reaction of your parents when you told them?

I often hear from my clients that when they told their parents they wanted to become a vet, a hairdresser, a garbage collector, a dancer, or an actor, the reaction was negative. They didn't take them seriously or disapproved of the idea. They had much better plans in mind for their daughters or sons, protecting them and pushing for a more financially secure and stable future.

Parents often do that with the best of intentions, not realizing what a profoundly negative impact such a reaction can have on their kids.

From this negative reaction from the most important people in our lives, we learn that our dreams are not important, wrong or frowned upon. We learn that our intuition and instinct to choose from the heart is not good. One of the most important things a child needs is the attention and approval of his/her parents. So when we learn that what we feel and dream of is not approved of, we stop feeling and start THINKING about what we could do to make our parents happy. That is when we start to use our rational brain above our feeling or intuition.

Our biggest job in regaining our passion is to learn to listen to our heart and intuition once more.

How do we do that?

The way I like to explain this is that we do it by connecting to our creative inner child. Our creative inner child is free. Free of the expectations of others. It loves to play, loves to be outside, loves to get dirty, is egocentric and egotistic and yet pure and unspoiled.

» When do you feel free?

_____

_____

» What do you do that brings joy and creativity into your life? Is it when you exercise? By being in nature?

_____

_____

One of the best exercises to connect to our passions and dreams is an exercise in creative writing. You need to first connect to your "creative child". So go for a walk, meditate, play with your kids, dance or do some exercise. Immediately after that, when you are still connected to your creative side, take a notebook and start writing.

» What do I like, what do I love?

_____

_____

» What makes me feel alive?

_____

_____

» What am I passionate about?

_____

_____

Just write, write, write. Do not edit. Do not judge.

Write everything that comes up. Do not block anything. If negative things come up, write them down too. Be free!

The more often you do this exercise, the better you become at it and more creative ideas will come up.

Exercise: Create your passion mood board

This is a very popular way to get to the essence of things really quickly. Many different businesses use this method. I did it with my husband when we were decorating our first house together. I also did it when I was starting my own business. I often do it with my clients when we start working on the topics of passions and mission.

But what exactly is a mood board? It is a collage of pictures, drawings, words and call-outs that illustrate an idea or concept.

Working with images means that you are using the right part of your brain, which is responsible for your emotions. The left part of our brain is the logical one. The right part of the brain always reacts before the left. That's why it is important to follow your first impulse. When you start to have second thoughts, your logical, left-brain thinking has kicked in. As you want to reveal your subconscious, you need to react to the first impulse otherwise the left brain will censor it.

DIY

To create your own mood board, flick through a stack of your favorite magazines. Cut or tear out images or words that catch your attention for whatever reason. Do this for at least 30 minutes. The idea is to have at least 20 to 30 pictures that you can use to create your mood board. Once you have collected the images, arrange them on a table or on the floor. See if there is a story line or certain themes in those pictures. Then take a big piece of paper and glue the images to it.

Once you are done, take another look at your mood board and decide on one word that describes each picture for you, or the reason you have selected it. What does this picture represent for you? Write that down on the picture or next to it.

After that, have a look at your mood board with fresh eyes or ask a friend/partner to have a look with you.

» What does each of you see?

_____

» What are the main themes?

_____

» How do you feel when you look at your mood board?

_____

» What does your mood board tell you about your passions?

_____

» What does your mood board tell you about YOU?

_____

The alternative "online" way of doing this exercise is to use Pinterest. If you do not have an account, you need to create one. Create a new board, which you will call "My passions" or "My mood board" and follow the same steps as in the exercise above.

Other ways of discovering your passion

Look at your hobbies

One of my favorite hobbies is reading. I love books. I love buying books. My husband gets a bit fed up, as I buy at least 10 new books every month. I used to buy only physical books, but when I was living in Mexico I had to wait for weeks for some, so I started to order ebooks. Nowadays, I decide which books I want to have a hard copy of and which I can live with in ebook format.

The subjects of the books are revealing. I love self-development, self-help, psychological books, and I always have — long before I decided to change my career.

So if you also love to buy books, look at the subject matter. It will tell you a lot about your passions.

Not all your hobbies will turn into your passions and not all your passions will make your career, but some might! I also love cookbooks, but I know I am never going to make cooking my profession. But you might!

So make a list of the common subjects of the books you are reading. The same counts for magazines.

If you are not into reading, what do you like to do when you have free time? Do you like sport? What types of sports? What does it tell you about your hobbies and passions?

Here is a list of the most popular hobbies and interests. Mark yours, and add any others that come to mind.

Books	Volunteering	Traveling
Reading	DIY	Yoga
Acting	Handcrafts	Running
Theater	Knitting, crocheting	Biking
Cinema	Sewing	Swimming
Art	Working with wood	Horse riding
Foreign languages	Sculpture	Team sport
Psychology	Photography	Cooking
Self-development	Gardening	Healthy eating
Spirituality	Fishing	Food
Writing	Nature	Music
Toys	Ocean	Singing
Women's rights	Animals	Playing an instrument
Minority rights	Plants	Dancing
Human rights	Bird watching	Antiques

History	Start-ups	Social media
Decor	Social start-ups	Web design
Design	Money	Internet
Fashion	Investing	Communities
Home decoration	Innovation	Developing countries
Business	Cars	Health

Once you have selected your favorite topics, take a big piece of paper and write them all down. See if you can cluster them. Then check whether you can refine them. For example, if you are interested in nutrition, what aspects are you particularly interested in? Is it healthy food for babies, nutrition for athletes, diets for those with cancer?

What subjects are you passionate about?

Very often our interests are based on our life experiences. Think about the experiences that have had an impact on you. Are there any links to your favorite topics?

Are there some topics you tend to read more about than others? Which topics occupy your mind every day?

Look into your childhood

Our interests manifest in early childhood, just as our talents do. As a child, I often knitted clothes for my dolls, and knitting is still one of my hobbies. I also loved playing school with my younger sister and two cousins. I was the oldest of the four of us and I was always the teacher. I loved to explain things to them. I remember it like it was yesterday. But it only came to me recently, when I was reflecting on many of these exercises while writing this book. Since I started my coaching business, I have also been training and holding workshops, and I really like this part of my job. I love to explain theories and concepts — to transfer my knowledge.

Now when you look back at your childhood activities, what did you play at, what were you interested in? Have a look at the Talents chapter again. What did you write down there? The earlier the memory, the better.

A lot of my clients think that when we focus on their passions or talents, they will discover some magic, external thing that they have never thought about. Most of the time it is not a journey outside, but a journey inside. However, the way it is shaped also very much depends on external circumstances. Using the analogy of a raw diamond, you have to find it first, but then to optimize its price, you need to cut and polish it in the best possible way.

The purpose of this part of the book is for you to find your raw diamond, the diamond within you. Only once you have found it, can you cut it and shape it the way you want to. We will do this in the last chapter of this section and in the third part of the book.

Look for your raw diamonds! If you haven't found your raw diamonds, there is nothing to shape! Don't worry at this stage if you do not know exactly how you will shape them.

What if I cannot discover my passion?

"Your work is going to fill a large part of your life, and the only way to be truly satisfied is to do what you believe is great work. And the only way to do great work is to love what you do. If you haven't found it yet, keep looking. Don't settle. As with all matters of the heart, you'll know when you find it."
Steve Jobs

Passion is not something that you can discover in a purely theoretical way. A lot of my clients who want to discover their passion ask, "How do I know if this is THE passion? How can I be sure of that?" Well, until you try it out in practice, you cannot be sure. When I was working as an accountant, I knew that this was NOT my passion. Although I did not know it at the time, when I was trying out different things, I was actually looking for my passion. The most serious attempt was when I did a one-year classical massage course. I liked the idea of helping people and I guess I was attracted by the fact that it was completely out of my comfort zone. However, by doing the course I discovered that this was not the right path for me. But could I have known that upfront? No, probably not. Not everything in our lives can be resolved in our heads; it requires real life experience — you need to feel it in your bones to know whether you love something or not.

So identify the things that interest you and start taking action on finding out if any of them have the potential to become your passion. It will be a path of trial and error, but there is no other way.

Conclusions

"In doing something, do it with love or never do it at all."
Mahatma Ghandi

So now please take time reflect on this chapter and form conclusions about what you have learned about yourself.

My passions are:

_____

_____

What do these passions mean for my career? What changes do I need to make in my career in order to fully embrace my life mission?

_____

_____

What have I learned about myself and my career in this chapter?

_____

_____

What ideas do I have now about the direction in which I want my career to grow?

_____

_____

Have I started to see a pattern?

_____

_____

Chapter Nine

Where? Your ideal workplace

"If you want light to come into your life,
you need to stand where it is shining."
Guy Finley

For some of us it is more important to work in a prestigious company rather than in the right job. For others, it is the other way round. And of course it is not necessarily a case of one way or the other; combining both options is a dream for many of us.

Sometimes starting to work in a great company may mean that you will not be in your dream position right away, but it can open the doors to many possibilities.

My first job after I graduated was at an Internet start-up run by two Australians. It was fun but after a year I knew I was ready for a move as the company was too small for me. Through a friend of my mother, I got an offer of a job as an office manager at a company that was just entering the Polish market but was well known outside our country. I remember that I hesitated for some time, as I knew I could do so much more.

I decided to look beyond this position as I was assured that the company was going to grow fast, and had plenty of opportunities for growth, should I be as good as I claimed I was. I decided to give it a chance. I made it clear to my boss that I wanted to move as soon as the office had been set up. After a year, I was offered the choice of two different departments: commerce or finance. I chose finance as it was in line with my ambitions at the time. I ultimately wanted to become a CFO.

Although I decided years later that becoming a CFO was not the path that I wanted to follow, deciding to take a job that was not on the list of my dream jobs paid off big time!

I always tell my clients that they need to compile a list of dream companies that they want to work for. That list helps you to focus on what you want. Something in the company, organization, or environment that you would choose to work for should be in line with your vision, values, and mission.

In this chapter we will take a closer look at the specific environment you want to work in. There are so many choices. You could choose to work for yourself, in the corporate world, in academia, at a start-up, in a social enterprise, at an NGO, in healthcare, and so on. When I first arrived in the Netherlands, I remember visiting Keukenhof, the most beautiful gardens I have ever seen. I realized then how important environment is for me. I told my husband — my boyfriend at the time — that I wanted to look for a job in the finance department at Keukenhof.

One of my clients reflected the following on this aspect of the career search: "The 'Working Environment' exercise allowed me to realize, in black and white, why I was so uncomfortable in my current job. It just wasn't meeting many of the requirements that are important to me on HOW and WHERE to work. This made me realize two things:

a) Putting a precise name to the discomfort made it easier to bear. It helped to know that I wasn't happy there because I needed to be listened to more, to have more opportunities for growth, to be in an environment of professional rigor, and to have freedom to act. Now I knew what to focus on, exactly where the itch was coming from and why it bothered me, instead of hating all eight hours of the job, my colleagues, and our business partners. It relieved a lot of anxiety.

b) It made me realize how much the how and where matter to me at work. It almost felt that, within limits, what I was working on didn't matter, as long as I was doing it my way. I had been considering going back to the private sector (even if I hadn't enjoyed it as much as NGO work), just to fulfill these meaningful elements in my working environment. The feeling of wanting to go back to the private sector scared me; it made me feel like I was betraying my mission to help others, like I was giving up. Once I understood that this impulse came from a need to have certain elements present in the way I work, I could understand this impulse better, and realized that it wasn't me swinging from one side of the spectrum to the other (again), it was just me looking for a place where I fit."

Values and environment

For the purposes of this chapter, you need to look at your core and work values again. These values will guide you towards discovering the type of working environment that fits you best.

So go back to the chapter on values to remind yourself what they are, and what they tell you about your current workplace. Is it a good match? If so, why? If not, why not? Which values are not being met?

Two very important values of one of my best friends are freedom and adventure. This desire for freedom is expressed in being able to decide what to do at work and taking responsibility for his decisions. For him, adventure means working in countries that often operate in grey areas — where things are fluid and open to interpretation. Another important value for him is receiving appreciation from others. He was happy working in one of the top positions at an international company in Argentina where he enjoyed a lot of freedom, and was appreciated, if not adored. Then he was offered a top position at a company in Germany. Their management wanted him really badly. He felt appreciated, and enormously flattered, so without giving his values a second thought, he accepted the offer and moved across the ocean. But within the first week, he knew he had made a poor decision. How could he have been so blinded? He found himself in a stiff German company, where values like freedom and adventure were replaced with rules and hierarchy. For a couple of months, he really suffered. Luckily a new job offer came around, this time in Romania. So he packed up and moved again. This time it was a very good decision. He was able to thrive again as his values of freedom and adventure were fully honored. It became clear that values like status and stability were very low in importance for him.

The impact of your values on different components

Type of work ownership

- » Self-employment: Working for yourself, developing/selling your own products or services
- » Self-employment: Working for yourself as a consultant (hiring your services out temporarily at other companies)
- » Self-employment: Working in a partnership (working closely with someone else)
- » Full-time employment: Being a full-time employee
- » Combination of self-employment and employment: Working part time (for example, partly in your own company, partly being employed)
- » Volunteering
- » Various combinations of the above

Look at your core and work values and see what they tell you about your preferred type of employment. If your top values are independence and flexibility, this might point you in the direction of self-employment. However, if your values are safety and stability, starting out on your own is probably not the best option.

If I look at my own work values, flexibility is one of my top values. But after working alone for many years, I realized that I miss the team spirit of my previous work — the feeling that we are united in achieving a common goal, the feeling that we can rely on each other. This value is, however, not strong enough to get me back into full-time employment, but it has given me a clear indication that things need to change in my company. This is one of the reasons I started to collaborate with various freelancers. I decided to outsource things that I could have done myself. I hired a virtual assistant to help me with my website and hired consultants to work on various projects. In the past, I have worked with interns. I also work with a business coach. This gives me the feeling of teamwork and satisfies this need to some extent.

Size of the company

Your values and preferences will also tell you what size of company fits you best.

Small	up to 50 employees
Medium	up to 250 — 1,000 employees
Big	above 10,000 employees
Multinational	
Local versus international versus global	

Working hours

How do you want to structure your day? How many hours a day do you want to work?

Before I became a mother, like many of us, I was working 40+ hours a week and I was traveling half the time. Two weeks in the Netherlands (my home base), two weeks in the US, two weeks in the NL, one week in Austria, two weeks NL, two weeks Belgium, three weeks in the NL, two weeks in Australia and so on. In almost four years, I had visited many, many different countries.

But when I became a mother, I decided to stay at home with my daughter for a year. A lot of my girlfriends went back to work when their babies were three or four months old and they had stressful 40-hour workweeks. I knew I could not and did not want to do it. Not for my baby and not for myself.

I probably work more than 40 hours a week now, but I work when I want to work. I can pick up my daughter from school every day and I can go back to work in the evening when my husband is home. Flexibility is still one of my main prerequisites as far as my work schedule is concerned.

Of course, when you choose to be employed, flexibility can become an issue, but it doesn't have to be. One of my good friends who has a senior position at a multinational company has a home-office contract. She told me that she often works in her pajamas. When she became a mother it was even more important not to have to sit at the office from nine to five.

> » How many hours a day and on which days would you like to work, ideally?
>> part-time
>> full-time
>> home-office

Commuting: Distance from home

One of the other elements in creating an optimum working environment is this: literally how far are you prepared to go? How long you sit in a car, train, and plane has a huge impact on the other aspects of your life, like family, hobbies, and wellbeing.

A couple of my clients have consciously rejected certain companies because they do not want to sit in traffic for three hours a day. If you do the math, three hours a day equates to 15 hours a week, 60 hours a month, and 600 hours a year (and I have given you two months of holidays). And that adds up to almost 25 days a year! Almost a month!

Company's values and mission

What are the values of the company and what is its mission?

Sometimes we want to work for certain companies just because they sell a product you love, deliver a service you are crazy about, or are simply doing things you support. Sometimes it's about the way the company runs its operations. Or simply because you think it is cool — think of Google or Apple.

A couple of months ago, I read *Delivering Happiness*, in which Tony Hsieh, CEO of the online shoe and clothing company Zappos, shares the success story of the company but also its mission and values. If you haven't read it, I strongly recommend that you do.

After I read it, I thought, "Wow, what a great place to work at," because their values and the way they run the company really resonated with me. This is a great example of how the "where" and "who" can matter much more than the "what". The company's main business is selling shoes online. I have to admit, I have no interest in shoes — pretty unusual for a woman, but true. Still, the example of a truly great working environment, where the company values were really followed and people really mattered, gave me a lot to think about.

Another example of a great company, in which the "where" and "who" are more important than the "what", is TOMS Shoes. The business model, which embraces the company's mission "One for one", made a huge impression on me. The company provides a pair of shoes to a poor child for every pair of shoes it sells. In this example, it is the "why", the company's mission, that resonates strongly with me.

Desired industry

If you have done the exercise from Chapter Eight, "What? Your passions", it will be much easier to come up with your list of desired industries. Once you have looked at the values and mission of a company you may decide to exclude it from your list of dream companies.

Working environment (rooms, open space, international, local etc.)

If you could design your immediate environment — things like your workspace and desk — what would it look like? Is it inside or outside, is it a small room where you sit alone, a big room where you sit with others, or a huge open space. Based on our personality type — introvert or extrovert — we have different needs.

What does introversion or extroversion actually mean? According to Swiss psychiatrist and psychoanalyst C.G. Jung, introversion and extroversion are the ways people gain or lose energy. People who are introverted get energized when they are on their own and lose energy when surrounded by many people. For extroverts, the opposite applies; they gain energy from contact with people and lose energy when alone. They need to charge their batteries through contact with others.

Knowing whether you are more extroverted or introverted can have a huge impact on selecting your environment. Imagine that you are an introvert and you have to sit in a big room full of people talking on the phone, all day, every day. You would be exhausted! Of course, even extroverts need quiet time to sit and focus on difficult work, just as introverts need and like contact with others.

Take this quiz to help you determine whether you are an introvert or an extrovert.

Introversion	Extroversion
[ ] I like to reflect	[ ] I like to interact
[ ] I have a few very close friends	[ ] I have a big group of friends

[ ] I think first, then act   [ ] I act first, then think

[ ] I like to be by myself   [ ] I am at my best when in a big group

[ ] I am at my best in a   [ ] I prefer to be surrounded
small group of friends   by others

[ ] I get energy from my inner   [ ] I get energy from the outside
world   world

Now it is time to write down YOUR favorite working conditions. But before you do that, think about which conditions are more important than others. They probably do not all carry the same weight. It depends on your personal situation and your current life stage. This means that it could and most certainly will change within the next few years.

When I look at my own requirements from a couple of years ago to now, they are completely different. When I was single, I did not care how long I would have to commute or how many hours a week I worked. I just knew I wanted to work in a fast-paced international company. When I became a mother, my perspective changed completely. It did matter how long I spent at work and how long it was going to take me to get there. And I did care about the purpose of the company.

Creative ways to find your ideal work setting

Exercise 1: Draw your ideal workplace

As mentioned before, drawing forces us to use a creative part of our brain, which is related to intuitive thinking and emotions. So if you have trouble writing down your answers, it is a great alternative.

Exercise 2: Visualize your ideal workplace

You can do this exercise with a friend. Ask your friend to ask you questions about the workplace while you sit with your eyes closed. It works similarly to the exercise above. After the visualization is complete, write down what have you seen.

Exercise 3: Create a mood board of your ideal workplace

This is the same exercise as the one on your passions but this time it focuses purely on the workplace. Go through various magazines and select indoor and outdoor images that resonate with you. Put them on a big sheet of paper and take a moment to reflect on what you see. Ask yourself have why you selected the pictures you did, and what they mean to you. Try to describe what every picture represents.

Other great ways

Exercise 4: Top 30 companies

Even if you are considering working for yourself, this is a great exercise. Think of the companies (big and small) that inspire you. Next to every name, write down one word that describes the reason you chose this company. Do you see any patterns?

This list will also provide you with a clear focus on where you want to move to from where you are. You now have your ideal situation written in black and white.

Conclusions

So now please take time reflect on this chapter and form some conclusions about what you have learned about yourself.

What are the most important requirements regarding my work environment?

_____

_____

What do these requirements mean for my career? What changes do I need to make in my career in order to fully embrace these aspects?

_____

_____

What have I learned about myself and my career in this chapter?

_____

_____

What ideas do I have now about the direction in which I want my career to grow?

_____

_____

Have I started to see a pattern?

_____

_____

Clients' Stories

Yoli

"I realized that I knew deep down that I needed to make a major change, but I was too scared to admit it. It felt less risky to 'throw tantrums' at my job than to take responsibility and work towards some real change."

I was working for an international NGO on HIV prevention. I had been working on more or less the same project for over five years, and I was feeling a bit conflicted. On paper, I was living a dream: helping people in a cool organization, traveling for work and living in Europe for my job (I'm from Mexico), but I didn't feel really fulfilled. I was frustrated with the dynamics. Yes, NGOs might look like the perfect place to work, but they are like any other! I felt as if I wasn't in the right place and that I needed to move on but I didn't know what step to take, and even questioned my commitment to social causes, which I had taken as a given.

The Netherlands is very different from Mexico. I was in a serious relationship with someone from the Netherlands, so I was very much installed there, but without much of a network to support me. Any possibility of change, unless it was to a completely safe spot, was very scary.

I decided to follow the coaching process because I was unhappy, and didn't know what else to do. A change was mandatory, but I didn't know what to change to, and I was scared of the implications. Of course, I discussed this with my partner and friends, but it didn't seem to take me anywhere, and the frustration seemed like it was there to stay. In hindsight, I think I knew somewhere within me that a big change was needed; I was feeling overwhelmed and didn't know how to proceed.

What I wanted from coaching was to have a clear idea of the steps I needed to take, and to feel better about my professional life. I found that — at least for me — problems like these stop mattering when I start taking action to solve them. I don't need to have completed a career change to feel better about myself, just taking the first steps makes a big difference and gives me energy. I was feeling lost and wanted to regain direction.

I remember meeting Dorota at a fair for expats in Amsterdam. I don't recall the exact moment I decided to call her. I think it was more that I had already made the decision to get help, then Dorota showed up so I grabbed the opportunity. In our meetings, which took place every two weeks, she asked me different questions and proposed different exercises, to get to know myself better, clarify my preferences, and identify where the "sticky" points were.

The two exercises that I found most impactful were the "Working Environment" exercise (page 164) and the "Parent-Adult-Child model" (page 229).

The "Working Environment" exercise allowed me to see, in black and white, why I was so uncomfortable in my job. The tasks themselves or the general mission might be great, but if I'm not in the right environment, I feel frustrated.

In fact, as I look back on my time at the NGO, I realize that for me, it's not so much about WHAT the work is, but HOW I work. It almost felt as if what I was working on didn't matter at all (within limits), as long as I was doing it my way. I've been happy doing Excel crunching and human resources, and reviewing social programs. It works as long as certain things that are important to me are in place: independence, a sense of purpose, intellectual challenge, and stimulating colleagues. If I lose these, it doesn't matter what I'm doing, I just feel like I need to move on. Now, in my job searches, I pay a lot of attention to this aspect and it has helped me make a couple of big decisions that I think were positive.

A part of me had been considering going back to a private company (even if I didn't enjoy it as much as NGO work), just to fulfill these needs. That feeling (of wanting to go back to the private sector) scared me. It made me feel like I was betraying my own mission to help others, and that I was giving up. Once I knew that this impulse came from a need to have certain elements present in the way I work, I realized that I wasn't being fickle; I was just looking for a place that was a good fit for me. My desire for freedom of time and of action indicated some sort of need to work independently.

I now know what to focus on; I know exactly where the itch is coming from and why it bothers me. It has relieved a lot of anxiety. Just putting a precise name to the discomfort was comforting. Knowing that I wasn't happy there because I needed to be listened to more, to have more opportunities for growth, to be in an environment of professional rigor, and to have the freedom to act made a big difference.

The "Parent-Adult-Child model" (Chapter Thirteen) was tough to face, and I don't think I am done digging into all the implications it had for me. It was very helpful to realize that some of the aspects of a career that I thought were a must were actually external "rules" (from society, from my parents, and what is expected of a "good" career) that I had internalized. At the same time, I was rebelling against them because they didn't suit me. I learned to part from those acquired — and now useless — rules. I also learned (or, should I say, I am still learning) when to rebel, and when to be strategic. You could say I'm becoming more of an Adult, owning my own choices, and also being realistic about where I stand now in terms of what is possible to change immediately, and what will have to wait.

This model helped me recognize what the various inner voices wanted for me (fulfillment? immediate relief? security at any cost?), and allowed me to give them their rightful place. It helped me realize that I knew deep down that I needed to make a major change, but I was too scared to admit it. It felt less risky to "throw tantrums" at my job than to take responsibility and work towards some real change. We are all marked by our upbringing and past experiences, of course; I saw how I had internalized parental discourses to "play it safe" and "follow the road you are supposed to", which were clearly not consistent with my needs. Lastly, I realized that I was afraid of choosing. I felt that saying yes to one thing meant saying no to all the other possible options, which was paralyzing: I was closing off options! Realizing which areas I was happy with, and which not, and giving my heart some freedom to daydream without judgment made me realize that I do NOT want everything, and that I'm okay with saying a definite no to some things, as they will not make me happy.

After all this you would expect me to have made a major life change right away — to perhaps have founded my own company. In a way I did, but on a small scale. I needed something to provide the fulfillment I was missing, but I knew I wasn't in a position to give up my job just like that. So I picked something I liked, which was creating order, and worked towards starting a money-making hobby from this, to see what that felt like. It evolved into organizing people's inboxes, teaching them the best way to work with email, and helping them to be organized in their time and actions. And so a business idea was born: to be a kind of a personalized efficiency coach. I started working with people I knew, consulting occasionally, which was fulfilling. I have to admit, it didn't make me a millionaire, but it gave me a lot of what I needed at the time, including motivation and energy. It also helped me break the paradigm that I always had to be someone's employee, and allowed me to taste the sweetness of a job I loved so much that I could have done it for free. It took attention and pressure away from my day job, and all the insights I gained about myself changed my passive negativity to the hope that, at the very least, I was finding some sort of path that was fulfilling. All I had to do was fine-tune it.

So this mini-change, an experiment, allowed me to make larger changes with more certainty. With what I had learned about myself in the process, I was able to make a more rational decision about my professional future. Instead of applying for any job just to run away from my current situation, I decided to draw a path that would take me where I wanted. And I now had the emotional tools to do it. I knew more about my wants and needs, about my fears and about how the inner voices made the worst-case scenario look very real. I knew that it all had to be done within a reasonable framework to ensure financial security, but now it didn't feel as if all security was being stripped away just by considering quitting. Thankfully I also had the support of my partner, and I could think big.

As Dorota predicted, coaching is not a crystal ball that gives the ultimate answer. Through coaching I acquired the tools and a level of understanding of myself that enabled me to make better choices, and that's much more valuable and empowering than gazing into a crystal ball.

I think my biggest success was confronting my fear of change and of the "what ifs". I allowed myself to explore other avenues without feeling that I was betraying my profession. By understanding that people can be helped on many levels, I opened up more possibilities, and was able to make more solid professional choices that felt right.

I was open to the coaching process because I felt I needed it. But that doesn't mean it was an easy-peasy process. The most valuable coaching sessions were also the toughest. I was confronted with questions I didn't dare answer, or didn't know how to answer, or that I had never even asked. It took a lot of introspection to understand myself, to search for the reason that a question triggered a certain emotion, and it took a lot of effort and fairly painful poking to allow the truth to emerge. I was aware that Dorota wouldn't let me get away with half answers, and that giving half answers wasn't serving me anyway. There was no way to overcome a problem other than to push through.

My path then led to private consulting in social and political matters in Mexico, where social problems are very apparent and human needs are generally more basic than in Western Europe. I pursued this in the belief that the combination of the issues I would address and the way of working (as an independent consultant) would be more fulfilling, and allow me a reasonable degree of financial security. However, certain credentials are required to work in this industry, in this country, so I studied towards a related master's degree.

After four years in Mexico, my path diverged even further from the original and I'm even happier and more convinced that I'm heading in the right direction. I worked as a public policy consultant for a while, but found it much more interesting to be involved in the administration of the organization than the projects themselves, so I transitioned to a human resources position with a focus on organizational development and process formalization. I am about to finish an MBA, and my next step will be (in decreasing order of familiarity) to do HR and OD in another company, in a different industry; to work on exploring and launching other initiatives in the same environment; or to move to a more challenging position with broader scope. My need to be directly involved in social work has diminished, partly because I no longer think that the only way to help is to work in a not-for-profit; for-profits can do it too, if properly run. Also, this is partly because I also feel I can fulfill my need to be involved in social projects on the side, rather than setting the constraint that it has to be my main occupation.

If, like me, you have felt stuck for quite a while and have tried everything you can think of, ask for help. Read books, do the exercises, talk to people, and listen to your instincts. Different people need different kinds of support at different times of their life, so don't be afraid to ask until you feel that you are knocking on the right door. Be brutally honest and don't judge yourself. It might lead to some difficult choices (for me, this was returning to studying, and to Mexico), but the choices will feel right. If you are okay, everything else will be okay, and you will have the strength to figure things out. If you are unsure, uncertain, or just frustrated, you are not using your energy for advancement.

I hope this book brings to many others what coaching brought me!

Chapter Ten

Who? The right people

"You are the average of the five people you spend the most time with."
Jim Rohn

Who you work with is often as important as where you work or what you do. You spend a large portion of your time with them and they have a significant impact on you and your entire life — whether you like it or not.

In this chapter, we will focus on identifying the type of people you would like to work with. This will also provide hints as to where these people work so you can see if these are the places you might be interested in too. We often like people who resemble us.

The questions below are designed to help you identify the types and the qualities of people you enjoy being around.

» Who do you admire?

Name at least five people you admire and next to their names, write down why you admire them. What is their talent or the quality that makes you admire them?

Name	Talent/Quality

1. _____
2. _____
3. _____
4. _____
5. _____

» What type of people give you energy?

_____

_____

» What type of people are you drawn to?

_____

_____

John Holland, an American psychologist, created the world renowned theory known as the Holland Codes[3], which many career coaches and counselors use. The theory describes six vocational personalities and categorizes them into the following types: Realistic (Doers), Investigative (Thinkers), Artistic (Creators), Social (Helpers), Enterprising (Persuaders), and Conventional (Organizers). Partly based on this theory, I have added couple of different career types.

1. Intellectual careers (academia, research, journalists, many office jobs eg. marketing, operations etc.)

2. Careers in sport (football players, tennis players, swimmers, yoga teachers etc.)

3. Artistic careers (actors, singers, performers, writers, etc.)

4. Empathic careers (teachers, nurses, doctors, psychologists, counsellors, coaches)

---

3   The 1959 article "A Theory of Vocational Choice," published in the Journal of Counseling Psychology

5. Social careers (environmental activists, human/animal rights activists, NGO employees, etc.)

6. Careers based on work with own hands (sculptors, painters, carpenters, car mechanics, flower arrangers etc.)

7. Spiritual careers (priests, monks, spiritual teachers)

8. Entrepreneurial careers (business owners)

9. Power/Persuasion based careers (sales, politics, CEO and similar)

10. Analytic (math) based careers (actuary, accountant, auditor, bankers, IT etc.)

   » Describe your ideal boss.

   _____

   _____

   » Describe your ideal colleague.

   _____

   _____

   » Describe your ideal subordinate.

   _____

   _____

   » Describe your ideal client.

   _____

   _____

   » What qualities in people irritate you (privately and professionally)? Why?

   _____

   _____

» If you could swap jobs with anyone for a day, who would you choose and why?

_____

_____

» What character traits do you appreciate in others?

_____

_____

Conclusions

So now please take time reflect on this chapter and form some conclusions about what you have learned about yourself.

What are the three most important requirements regarding the types of people at my workplace?

_____

_____

What are the implications of these requirements for my career?

_____

_____

What changes do I need to make in my career in order to fully embrace these aspects?

_____

_____

What have I learned about myself and my career in this chapter?

_____

_____

What ideas do I have now about the direction in which I want my career to grow?

_____

_____

Have I started to see a pattern?

_____

_____

Clients' Stories

Lisa

"Life is too short to not have some aspect of what you love present in your professional career."

My first 28 years centered around living and working where I grew up, in New England. I am naturally curious, and an explorer, so I dreamed of traveling the world. I firmly believe the clichéd idea that once we are open, ready, and clear on what we ask for, the universe conspires to make that happen, often in ways we would never have expected.

I was working in corporate HR and was quite happy and successful. I also had a great boss who I consider a mentor to this day, but I still felt the urge to live abroad. A close friend connected me with an organization that offered me the chance to not only live abroad but to take on a senior role that was out of my comfort zone — a challenging, demanding role that I would eventually thrive in.

The company chose me as the face of their MBA programs in Asia. I had the amazing opportunity to travel around Asia Pacific, representing them at MBA fairs, panel discussions and alumni events. I also had a very clear sales target. And despite a lack of experience in setting up teams, I had to build a team of 50 recruiters. I do tend to throw myself into deep water and learn to swim afterwards! The first six months were a steep learning curve, but I enjoyed that period most!

After spending three years in Hong Kong, my boyfriend and I decided to take a leap of faith and leave our jobs to volunteer for an HIV/AIDS NGO in South Africa. This experience was incredibly humbling, and personally and professionally enriching.

As my boyfriend (husband-to-be) and I plotted our next moves, the financial crisis hit, so there were fewer opportunities than before. We decided to move to Amsterdam, the Netherlands, which we were both excited about. The main driver for the move was a work opportunity for him, so I had to play catch-up. It can be exciting, but it is also overwhelming to throw yourself into a new culture, language and location — and to find your way in a job market you know very little about. After identifying companies I felt aligned to and that were regarded as great places to work, I landed a role at the corporate headquarters at Philips International. I wanted to build and strengthen my learning edges (areas beyond my comfort zone) to become more versatile in my strengths and skill set, so I took a global project management back office role. My function at Philips was mostly project management oriented, and I learned that this was not my strength or passion, no matter how hard I tried.

This was when I decided to seek help to better understand and identify my strengths and weaknesses and be more connected to my passion and purpose. And I found Dorota. My ultimate goal was to find a new position in an organization or company I was better aligned with. I was still learning about the job ecosystem in the Netherlands.

I found every coaching session helpful, as I was intrinsically motivated to be there, and was open to the process. Having someone objective listen and advise was incredibly beneficial. The coaching involved working through exercises that helped me explore and reconnect to what it was I was passionate about.

We often take our innate abilities for granted, tending to downplay them. I did that. Being outgoing, personable, sales oriented, able to connect the dots, and a natural networker all came very naturally to me and because I also used these abilities in my professional roles, I thought, "Oh, that's just who I am." I wanted to focus more on building my project management skills and other tangible skills. Through coaching, I realized that for me to be happy and to thrive in my career, I needed to find a role that would enable me to use my innate talents — and to really own them — in addition to the hard skills. When I looked at my CV, I saw that at one point I had brought in sales of over USD 1,5 million.

I needed to learn how to recognize this in myself. I noticed that some of my female colleagues downplayed their achievements, as did I, whereas my male colleagues totally exaggerated theirs. The coaching gave me more confidence in my abilities and achievements. I also realized that I needed to focus on front-facing jobs. It became patently clear to me that I thrive in dynamic environments and get energy from working with people.

Thanks to the coaching, I identified the type of working environment that suits me. My position at Philips was very much focused on the back office, which was not the right position for me. This was a hard lesson. When you are hungry for a new job, you just want to land it, so you ignore the details. Of course you do not always have the luxury of waiting for a position that really suits you.

More than all this, coaching helped me transition out of the corporate sector and find an organization I had no idea existed but that was completely aligned with my values, beliefs, and optimum work environment. You could say I hit the jackpot. And it happened as a result of a very easy step in my coaching process: reaching out to people in my network who had contacts in spaces and industries I wanted to learn more about. As a result of the wonderful powers of LinkedIn, the first person I reached out to was a connection I did not know personally. I simply went to learn more about the Dutch ecosystem, but this led to me finding out about an innovative, cutting edge working environment. I remember walking into their offices and thinking, "Wow, check, check, check, great office environment, wonderful, inspiring people. This is the organization I would love to work for." But it didn't happen right away; they didn't have any positions open at the time. So I told the person I had the coffee meeting with, "When you are scaling up, I would love to be considered for future opportunities, especially in the role you have." I realize it might have been a bit aggressive, but I just loved the place. I kept in touch just to keep the dialogue open. As luck would have it, two and a half months after our first meeting, I got a call. And I landed a job that fitted me like a glove, at THNK School of Creative Leadership!

At the same time, I was in the running for roles at LinkedIn and Facebook. I really loved the idea of working for either company — I guess we Americans are quite brand oriented! But when I looked more closely at the functions, I had the feeling that they were not the best fit for me — and they were not in the Netherlands.

During one of our coaching sessions, Dorota asked me to stand on pieces of paper, representing each of the companies, and imagine what it would be like to work there. But I couldn't fully see myself in those positions. I chose THNK — the lesser-known startup that offered the function that was perfect for me. What's more, the organization itself is amazing!

As much as I wanted to get stronger in my areas of weakness, or in my learning edges, which were glaringly obvious in my role at Philips, coaching helped me realize that I was better off finding roles in which my strengths could shine. One of the exercises relating to this that stuck with me was writing with the hand I don't usually write with — my right hand — and describing my feelings. (Find it on page 102 "Warm-up exercise: Left hand, right hand".) This simple exercise resonated with me, making the point that I needed to focus on roles that work mostly with my strengths and skill sets.

It has been five years since my sessions with Dorota and I couldn't have asked to land up in a better organization or role. Although I did not know where the coaching journey would take me, I was struggling to put the puzzle pieces of my professional life together, and mapping my path with Dorota helped immensely.

During the coaching, I identified an extremely important piece of the puzzle: the type of people, especially my mentors, I wanted to work with. My big question was: "Who leads the organization? Am I aligned with them and, most importantly, am I inspired by them?" I believe that we work for people rather than for organizations.

When I started to work for THNK, I was not an expert in startups or in innovation. My skill set and talents were, however, an extremely good match in terms of what the role required. Certain aspects of the job were similar to my MBA admission job in Hong Kong, but at THNK I was much more involved with the candidates. I was talking to people who were at the height of their career, looking to move up to the next level or to make a transition. My role was to counsel them to make sure that the THNK program was right for them. But it was not just about hunting talent and finding interesting people. It was also about creating the right mix of participants in a given program, and about building the community around the organization. We had a set of criteria that we were looking for in a creative leader. It was fun, but challenging.

Life is too short to not have some aspect of what you love present in your professional career. Your job does not have to fully define you, but it should make you feel that you are a valued team member, and that the purpose of the organization is aligned with your values and beliefs. If this is not the case, then it's time to dive into the sometimes uncomfortable process of figuring out not only what areas interest you, but what you can bring to an organization that is unique and can help them grow. What problem will you help the organization to solve, if they hire you? If you feel stuck, start making small moves forward. Stay the course and stay true to who you are and what your heart desires. If I reflect on my dreams as an 18-year-old, of traveling the world and overcoming my fears, I am still connected to them, even though I did not always know how to realize them. I did not have an abundance of money, contacts or opportunity; I had to create it all myself. Along my journey of combining my passion for travel and adventure with my career, I met my husband. I am grateful to have my partner in crime, Richard, along for the journey! I would never have met him had I not taken a leap of faith and followed my inner compass to a foreign land and a foreign job. Pushing yourself into that uncomfortable space where you doubt your abilities is indeed where the magic happens!

Chapter Eleven

Putting the puzzle pieces together

"It's not about the pieces,
but how they work together."
Unknown

My career model

You have now completed the biggest chunk of the work. It is time to put all the pieces of the puzzle together.

Fill in the chart below based on the information you gathered in the previous exercises.

My values

_____

_____

_____

My work values

_____

_____

_____

My life mission

_____

_____

_____

My passions

_____

_____

_____

My favorite working environment

_____

_____

_____

My favorite type of people (I want to work with)

_____

_____

_____

Fill in your career model

For many of my clients, coming up with ideas for their dream job based on the elements they have identified is the most difficult part of the process. That is why I asked you previously to brainstorm ideas at the end of each chapter in the section *Conclusions*.

Brainstorm career ideas

Take out a big piece of paper. Write directly on it or, even better, use Post-It notes and write your ideas on them. First write down all the elements you have identified (values, talents, passions, life mission, workplace and people). Then write down all the ideas you have come up with so far.

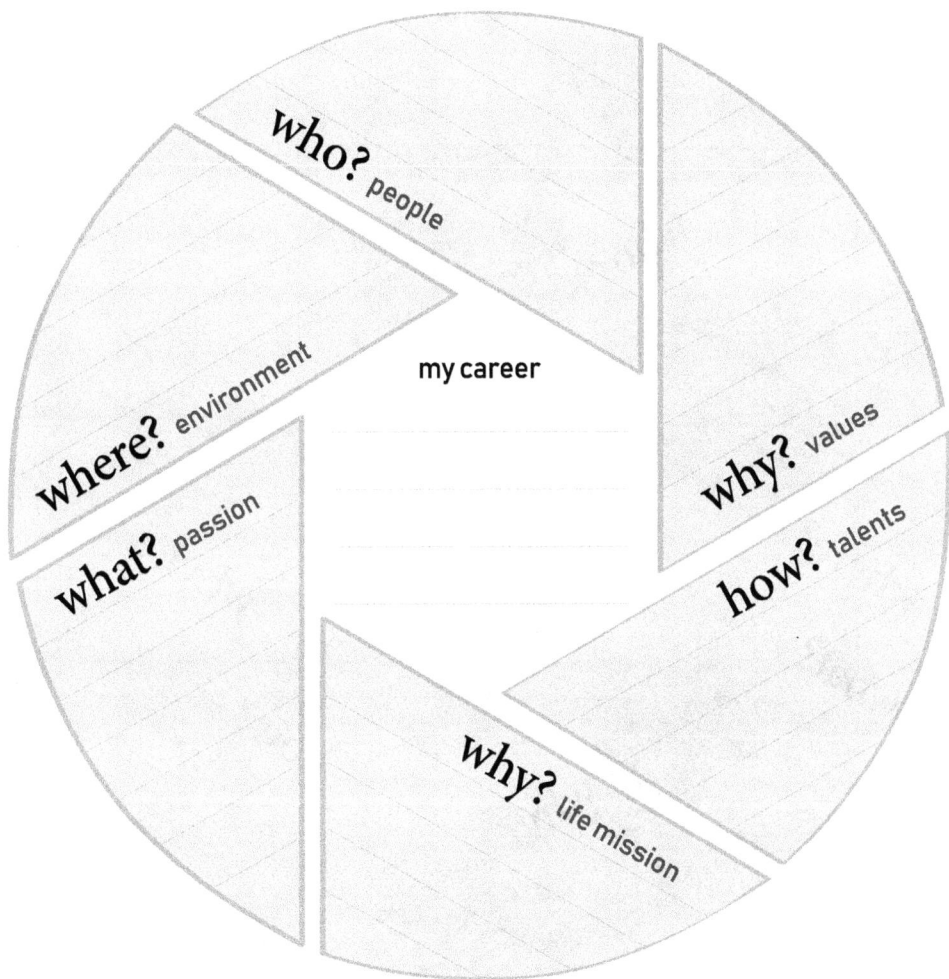

Amanda's career model

In order for you to see how others have done this, I have included the career model of one of my clients, Amanda. You can also read her full story at the end of this chapter on page 200.

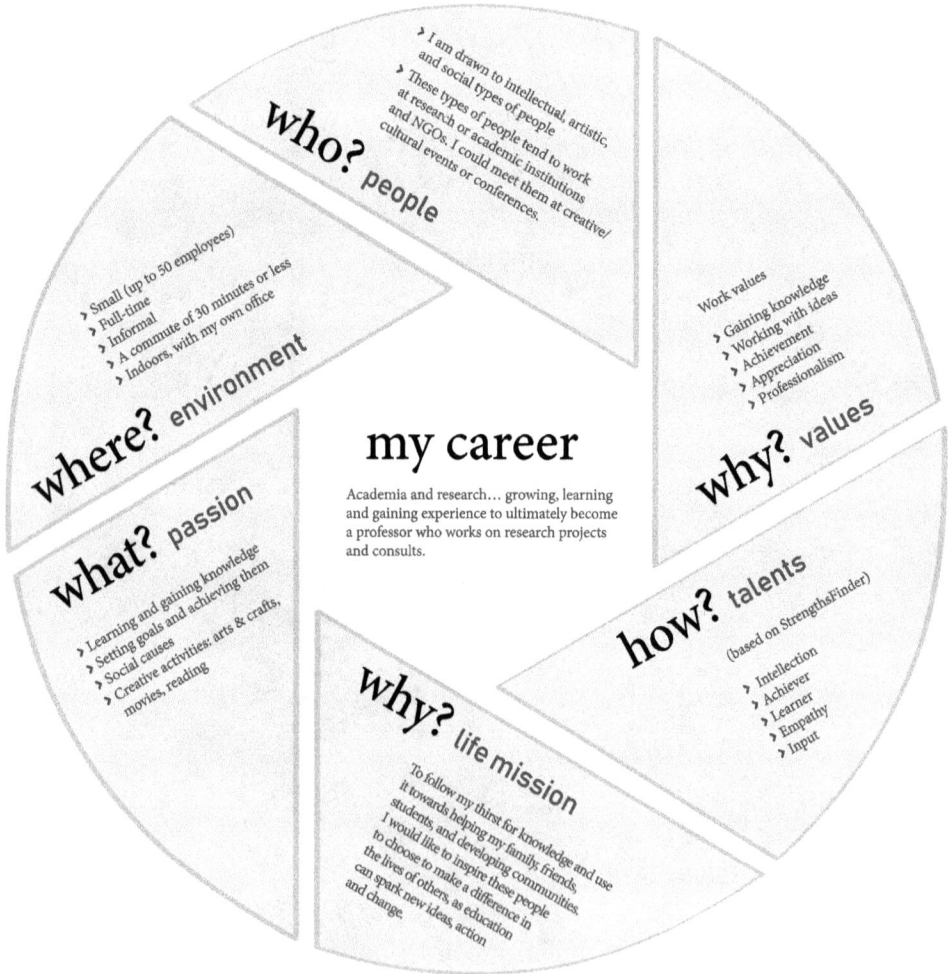

who? people
> I am drawn to intellectual, artistic, and social types of people
> These types of people tend to work at research or academic institutions and NGOs. I could meet them at creative/cultural events or conferences.

why? values
Work values
> Gaining knowledge
> Working with ideas
> Achievement
> Appreciation
> Professionalism

where? environment
> Small (up to 50 employees)
> Full-time
> Informal
> A commute of 30 minutes or less
> Indoors, with my own office

my career
Academia and research... growing, learning and gaining experience to ultimately become a professor who works on research projects and consults.

how? talents
(based on StrengthsFinder)
> Intellection
> Achiever
> Learner
> Empathy
> Input

what? passion
> Learning and gaining knowledge
> Setting goals and achieving them
> Social causes
> Creative activities; arts & crafts, movies, reading

why? life mission
To follow my thirst for knowledge and use it towards helping my family, friends, students, and developing communities. I would like to inspire these people to choose to make a difference in the lives of others, as education can spark new ideas, action and change.

Exercise: Career Model quiz

This exercise will help you to see the extent to which all the elements (values, talents, passions, life mission, workplace, and people) are present in your current job. At the end of each section, sum up the positive points. Write down the number, and then depending on the number, shadow the parts of the respective circles.

Example

Imagine that in the values section of the quiz, you marked three statements as true and five as false. That means you will shadow three out of eight pieces of the pie, as in the picture below. Please do it for all the sections. You will get a clear overview of where the painful points are hidden. Of course it is not realistic to expect to reach 100% in all areas. So do not worry; this exercise is an indication of the areas you need to work on first regarding your career.

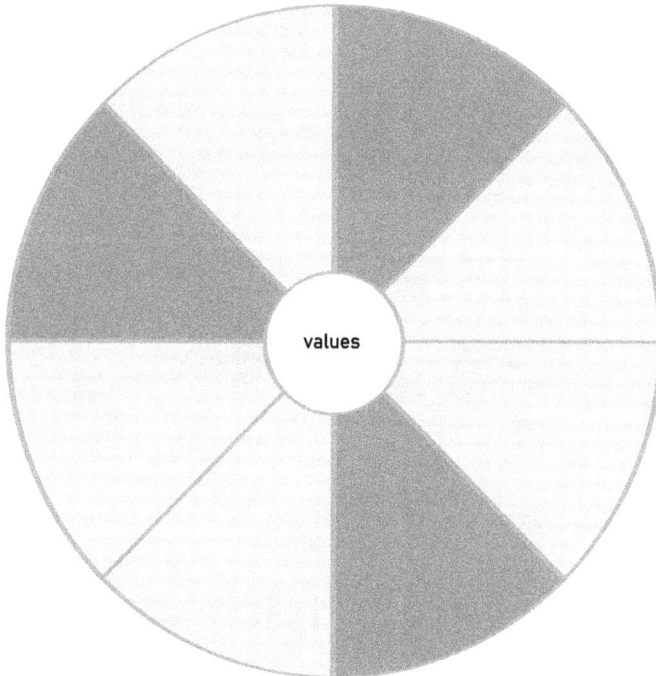

Now for each statement, mark if it is true for you, or false.

Values

True   False

Select your top 3 values and 3 work values and use them in the quiz below.

1. I honor .... (Core value 1) in my work.

[ ]   [ ]

2. I honor .... (Core value 2) in my work.

[ ]   [ ]

3. I honor .... (Core value 3) in my work.

[ ]   [ ]

4. I honor .... (Work value 1) in my work.

[ ]   [ ]

5. I honor .... (Work value 2) in my work.

[ ]   [ ]

6. I honor .... (Work value 3) in my work.

[ ]   [ ]

7. I feel that my boss respects my values.

[ ]   [ ]

8. I feel that my peers respect my values.

[ ]   [ ]

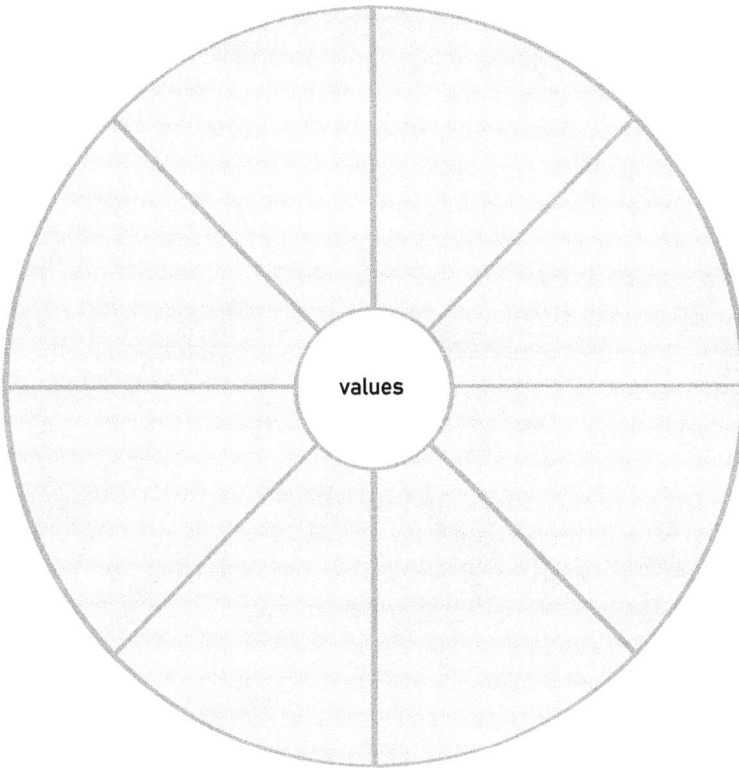

Talents

True   False

Select your top 3 talents and use them in the quiz below.

1. I use ...... talent at my work on a daily basis.
[ ]   [ ]

2. I use ...... talent at my work on a daily basis.
[ ]   [ ]

3. I use ...... talent at my work on a daily basis.
[ ]   [ ]

4. I use ...... talent on a weekly basis.

[ ]   [ ]

5. I use ...... talent on a weekly basis.

[ ]   [ ]

6. I use ...... talent on a weekly basis.

[ ]   [ ]

7. I am aware of my weaknesses and those I do not use more often than 30% of the time.

[ ]   [ ]

8. At work I am given enough opportunities to develop my talents.

[ ]   [ ]

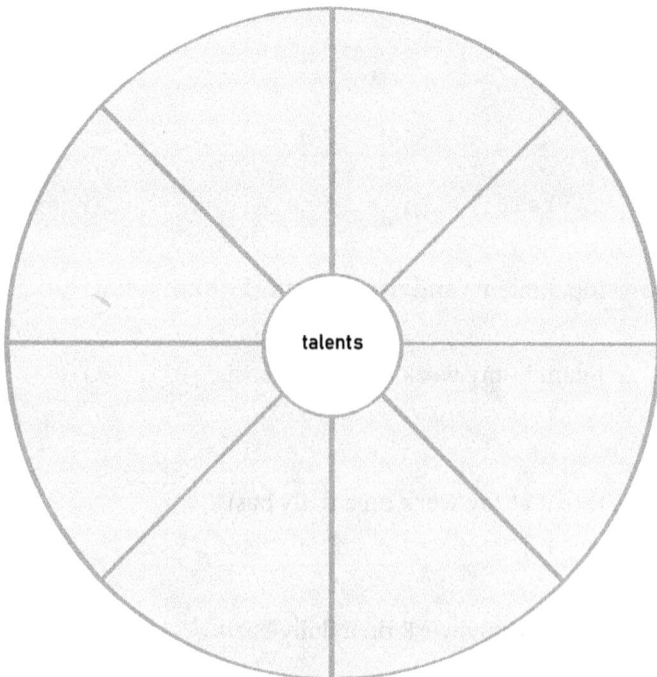

Life mission

True   False

1. I have a clear life mission.
[ ]   [ ]

2. I fulfill my life mission in my current career path.
[ ]   [ ]

3. I feel that in my life I contribute to people, organizations, or causes I believe in.
[ ]   [ ]

4. At my work I contribute to whom I want to contribute.
[ ]   [ ]

5. I value the mission statement of my company.
[ ]   [ ]

6. The mission statement of my company and my own mission statement are not contradictory.
[ ]   [ ]

7. I have a clear career plan that is in line with my life mission.
[ ]   [ ]

8. I feel that my life has a higher purpose.
[ ]   [ ]

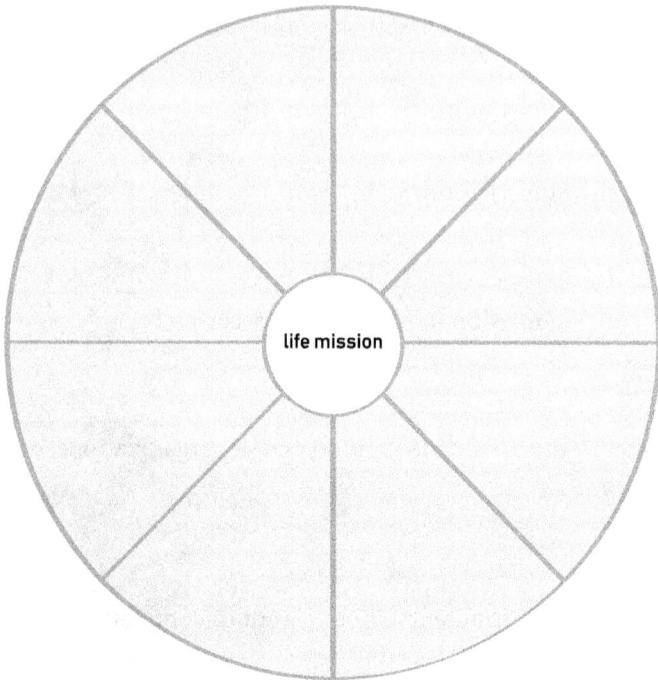

Passions

True   False

1. My job is in line with what I am interested in.
[ ]   [ ]

2. I do what I love and I love what I do.
[ ]   [ ]

3. My company's products/services are in line with my interests.
[ ]   [ ]

4. I am fully aware of my passions.
[ ]   [ ]

5. Outside of work I spend enough time developing my hobbies/passions.
[ ]   [ ]

6. I find the content of my job exciting.
[ ]   [ ]

7. I want to further grow in my area of expertise.
[ ]   [ ]

8. I spend enough time to learn more about things I am passionate about.
[ ]   [ ]

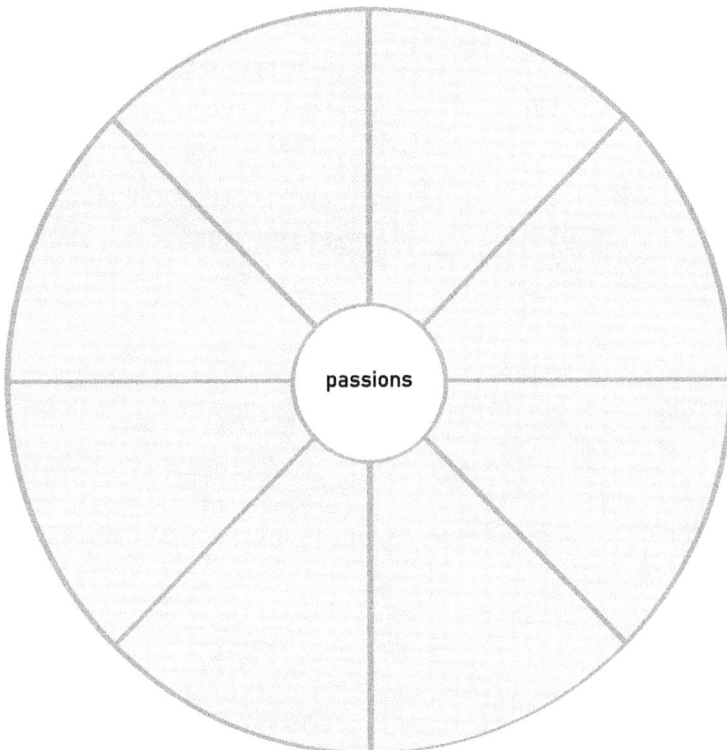

Environment

True   False

1. I feel good at my workplace.
[ ]   [ ]

2. I do not commute more than I wish to.
[ ]   [ ]

3. The size of the company suits my preferences.
[ ]   [ ]

4. I work as many hours as I wish (part-time/full-time).
[ ]   [ ]

5. The hierarchical structure (formal/informal) of the company suits my preferences.
[ ]   [ ]

6. The environment does not add stress to my work, which I would not be able to handle.
[ ]   [ ]

7. My work environment does not drain my energy.
[ ]   [ ]

8. In my daily life I spend enough time in my favorite environment.
[ ]   [ ]

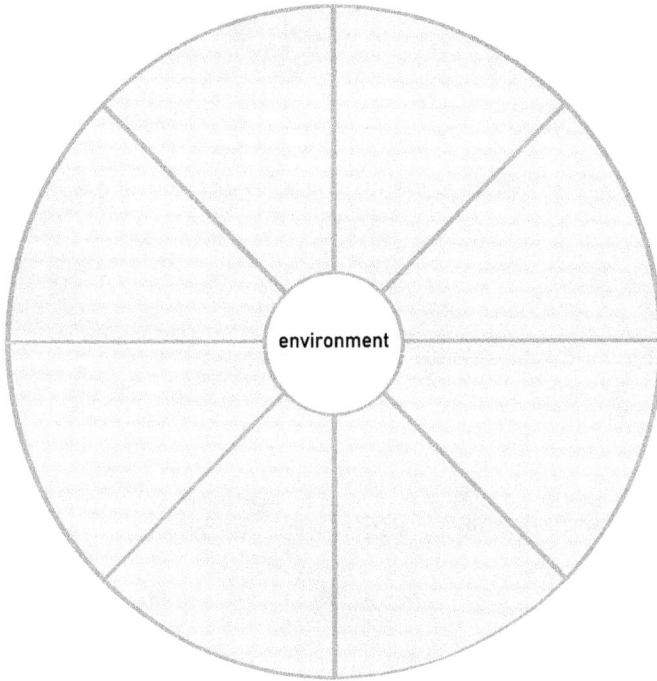

People

True   False

1. I know the type of people I click with.
[ ]   [ ]

2. At my work I am surrounded by people who think in a similar way I do.
[ ]   [ ]

3. At my work I am surrounded by positive people.
[ ]   [ ]

4. At my work I am surrounded by supportive people.
[ ]   [ ]

5. At my work there are people I know I can count on in difficult situations.

[ ]   [ ]

6. I do not work with people who drain my energy.

[ ]   [ ]

7. I have a good relationship with my boss.

[ ]   [ ]

8. I have a good relationship with my subordinates.

[ ]   [ ]

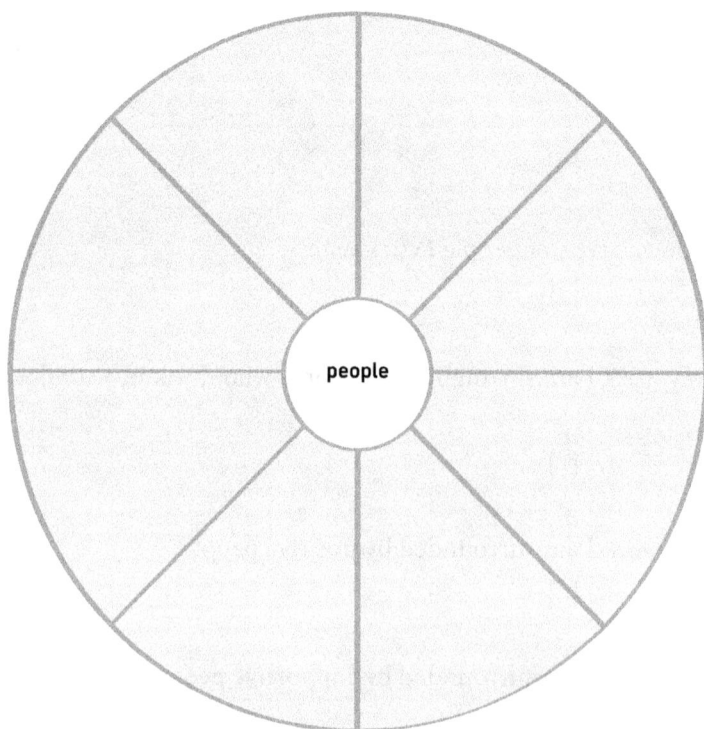

Careers under consideration

Now list down your top 3/5 ideas for your new career path.

1. _____
2. _____
3. _____
4. _____
5. _____

Clients' Stories

Amanda

"I have come to learn that I am often onto something when I feel the most vulnerable; the bigger the risk, the greater the reward."

I was an expat, working for a non-profit organization in the Netherlands. I wanted to make a decision about the next steps in my career and to feel happy with my choices. I was unsure about which sector, career path, and destination to follow. I followed the coaching process to gain perspective on what my next step would be.

Before I decided I needed coaching, I felt really lost and confused. I was sad that I was far from my family and friends, and I was frustrated because I was unhappy at work. I had many options for the next steps in my career: stay in the Netherlands, return home, or move to another country. I also debated the pros and cons of staying in the non-profit sector, going into the private sector, or pursuing an academic career. These options left me paralyzed, though. I did not know how to decide. I signed up for coaching with Dorota to help focus my decision-making and reasoning.

The two sessions that still resonate with me today are "Life Mission" (Chapter Seven) and the "Parent-Adult-Child model" (Chapter Thirteen). When I am making important decisions, I reflect on what it is that I truly want from life and evaluate whether my plans for the next steps contribute to my life mission. Also, when I am confused about a situation, or feel torn between what my head and my heart are telling me, I try to discern which part of me is "in the driver's seat". I think about the root of my concern in order to ground my decision-making in sound and rational thought processes.

I look back on my "Life Mission" every now and then to remind myself of my long-term goals, and to adjust them if necessary. The statement reminds me of my aspirations in life. The words that I wrote inspire me, and keep me motivated: "To follow my thirst for gaining knowledge and use it towards helping my family, friends, students, and developing communities. I want to inspire these people to want to make a difference in other people's lives. Education can spark new ideas, and inspire people's willingness and creativity towards action and change. I also want to have a family and a career that I am proud of. I want my family to grow and remain close. I also want my career path to be an excellent, inspirational, and admirable example for others."

The most difficult decision during the change process was whether or not to leave behind the life that I had created in the Netherlands. I felt like I was giving up, and that I had failed. But after talking it over with Dorota and reflecting, I realized that deep down I really wanted to be home, closer to my family and friends. When I thought about moving home, my mood was lighter, my voice was different, and my body felt less tense. I knew it was the right decision for me.

Also thanks to the coaching, I decided to pursue an academic career by undertaking a PhD degree.

My biggest success in the process was being accepted into the PhD program of my choice. I had considered applying to multiple programs at different universities to increase my chances but I decided that I wanted to go to one university in particular, so I only applied to that program. It was a bit scary, but I was very sure of my decision. I was overjoyed when I found out that I was accepted.

I have now completed the first year of my PhD program. I am back home, surrounded by my family and friends. I honestly cannot remember the last time I felt this healthy in every sense of the word. I feel mentally healthy, I am exercising and eating properly, I'm socializing, and I truly feel that I am doing what I am supposed to be doing in life.

The biggest take-away for me from my coaching process is that it is okay to be scared to make a big change in life. I have come to learn that I am often onto something when I feel the most vulnerable; the bigger the risk, the greater the reward.

My advice to others is this: when you feel stuck, that's when you know it's time to re-evaluate your situation and think about what it is that you really want from life and your career. I truly believe in the coaching process. It allows you to clear the cobwebs in your head that obscure your decision-making process. Talking out any problem not only allows you to gain perspective but also grants you some therapy. Just go for it!

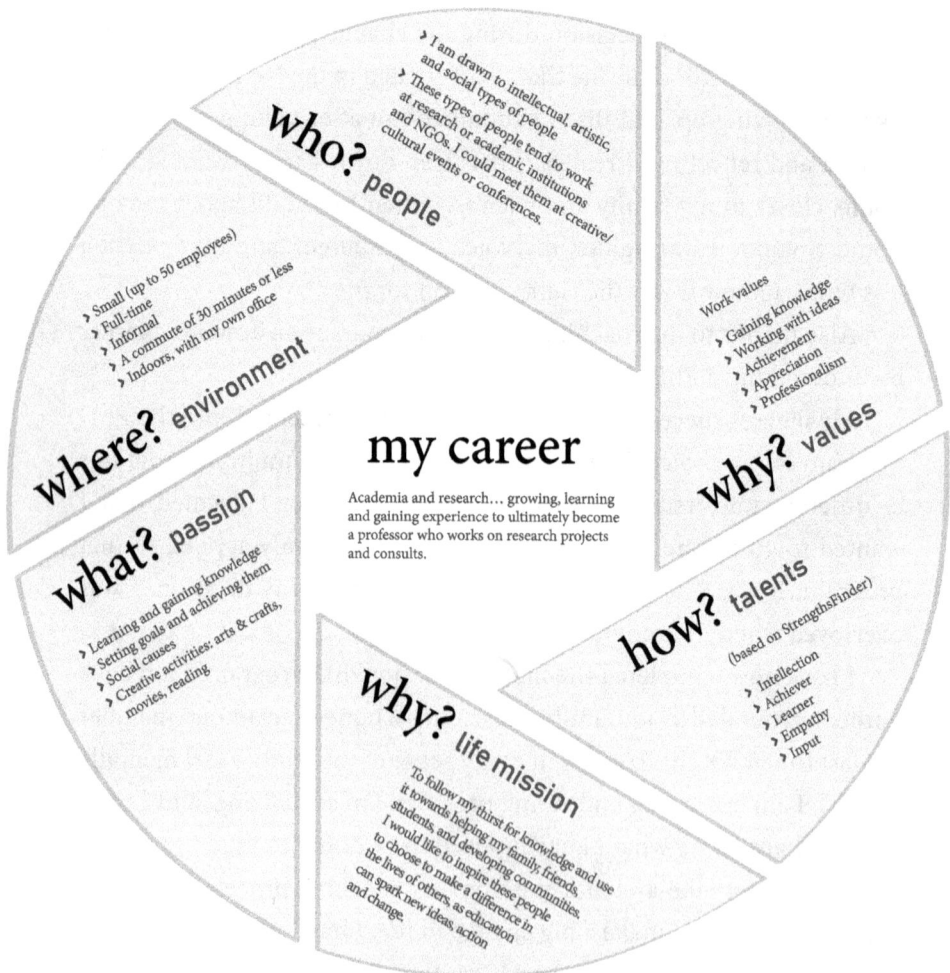

who? people

> I am drawn to intellectual, artistic, and social types of people
> These types of people tend to work at research or academic institutions and NGOs. I could meet them at creative/cultural events or conferences.

where? environment

> Small (up to 50 employees)
> Full-time
> Informal
> A commute of 30 minutes or less
> Indoors, with my own office

why? values

Work values
> Gaining knowledge
> Working with ideas
> Achievement
> Appreciation
> Professionalism

my career

Academia and research... growing, learning and gaining experience to ultimately become a professor who works on research projects and consults.

what? passion

> Learning and gaining knowledge
> Setting goals and achieving them
> Social causes
> Creative activities: arts & crafts, movies, reading

how? talents

(based on StrengthsFinder)

> Intellection
> Achiever
> Learner
> Empathy
> Input

why? life mission

To follow my thirst for knowledge and use it towards helping my family, friends, students, and developing communities. I would like to inspire these people to choose to make a difference in the lives of others, as education can spark new ideas, action and change.

Part III

The Transition

Chapter Twelve

Transition Plan

"A lot of people resist transition and therefore never allow themselves to enjoy who they are. Embrace the change, no matter what it is; once you do, you can learn about the new world you're in and take advantage of it."
Nikki Giovanni

This part of the book is about taking the big step from the drawing board to reality. But before you jump, there are still a few things to consider. Some of my clients have several career paths to consider, others have to choose from one or two options.

Career Paths

Write down your top three career paths. If you have only one path there is nothing to worry about — it just makes the process easier — but I would still recommend that you follow the steps below.

Career path 1

_____

_____

Career path 2

_____

_____

Career path 3

_____

_____

Analyze your potential career paths

Step 1. Gather data

Investigate the elements required to perform the new job. It is worth going into this activity in depth so that you understand whether the career path or job you have in mind really is something for you.

How do you actually gather the information? Here is a list of ways you can do this:

Internet research

This is a relatively easy way, especially for corporate jobs. Go onto job ad sites like monsterboard.com or LinkedIn and type in the function you are looking for. Make sure you collect at least five different job ads as the description of the functions might differ. Some recruiters give very brief requirements, while others go into more detail. The more information you gather, the better.

Talk to people who are already doing the job you want

This is a crucial point. I advise you to always include it in your research — especially if you are considering a big career change (like starting your own business, for example). People who are actually performing the job can give you lots of valuable information you will never find on the Internet.

Start your research close to home. Think of anyone you know who might be able to help. If you are currently employed, could you talk to a colleague who is already doing the job you want? Of course, this could be tricky, as you might not want others to know that you are thinking of making a change. It is up to you to make a judgment call.

But what do you do when you do not know someone personally in the career type you want? Be creative about using your network effectively. If you have an active LinkedIn account, do a search. Look for people with the job titles you are interested in to see whether any of your connections could help you to contact them. You could also use Facebook and Twitter. Post a message that you are looking for people with that job title or people who are already in the business you are thinking of starting.

Offline ways to connect with the right people

- ✓ Attend networking events and actively look for people with the desired job title.
- ✓ Ask your family, friends, neighbors, and colleagues — anyone you come across — if they know someone in the job you are interested in. Always explain the purpose; people like to hear the "why" and are generally supportive.
- ✓ Go to fairs related to the job you are interested in. For instance, if you want to start your own business and make your own cosmetics, attend health fairs or small business fairs in your town to meet people who are already in the business.
- ✓ Look for conferences in the industry that you are interested in.

Before you talk to any of the people you have found, prepare well. Ask specific questions about daily activities, tasks, talents, skills, experience and the knowledge necessary to perform the job. But, of course, you can ask so much more than that. Also remember to think about the questions through the filter of your values, talents, passions, and so on.

Potential questions you could ask

What do you like most about your job?

What do you dislike most about it?

What are the growth prospects on this career path?

What do you find most rewarding about this career?

What do you find most challenging?

Where do you want to go from here?

What are the daily activities you have to perform?

Once you have gathered enough data, you are ready for the following steps.

Step 2. Write down all the activities that you will have to perform in your future (potential) job.

When I think of my current job as a career coach, my activities are:

Daily
- ✓ Prepare sessions with clients, including sending emails and reading though the information provided by clients.
- ✓ Conduct sessions with clients, including actively listening to my clients, coaching and supporting them.
- ✓ Know how to apply certain models, theories, or exercises on the spot, based on the client's situation.
- ✓ Talk to potential clients.

Weekly
- ✓ Think of new content for articles.
- ✓ Invent and design new exercises for clients.
- ✓ Keep up to date on social media.
- ✓ Network online and offline.
- ✓ Keep financial administration up to date.

✓ Send offers to corporate clients.

✓ Work on projects: a book, website and online course.

Monthly

✓ Learn about and read new coaching or psychology related content (books, articles, magazines, workshops, training).

✓ Participate in various business development related workshops.

✓ Conceptualize, design and implement new programs for clients.

✓ Set and evaluate the monthly business strategy.

✓ Keep financial administration up to date.

Yearly

✓ Decide on a business strategy.

✓ Write a book.

Step 3. Analyze the following elements

Once you have written down all the activities you will have to perform in your new job, you need to break it up into talents, skills, experience, and knowledge.

Talents

Looking at the activities you will have to perform daily in your future job, which talents will you use to perform a given activity? On the left side I have put my example — the talents I need to perform my job as a coach. I did the same for skills, experience, and knowledge. On the right side you need to write down the talents, skills, experience, and knowledge you think you will need to perform your future job.

Dorota's example: **Talents I will need:**

✓ Empathy

✓ Influencing

✓ Convincing

- ✓ Synthesizing
- ✓ Learning
- ✓ Writing
- ✓ Intuiting
- ✓ Achieving
- ✓ Entrepreneurship

Skills

Looking at the activities you will have to perform daily in your job, think of the skills you will need to use to perform a given activity.

Dorota's example: **Skills I will need:**

- ✓ Communicating
- ✓ Questioning
- ✓ Interviewing
- ✓ Listening
- ✓ Language skills
- ✓ Motivating
- ✓ Supporting
- ✓ Giving feedback
- ✓ Selling

Experience

Based on the tasks you will have to perform, write down the experience that is necessary to perform the job.

Dorota's example: **Experience I will need:**

- ✓ Coaching, training, mentoring
- ✓ Business experience
- ✓ Working closely with people from different cultures and backgrounds

Knowledge

Based on your future function, write down the kind of knowledge that is necessary to perform the job.

Dorota's example:	**Knowledge I will need:**
✓ Coaching education	
✓ Various short courses related to communication, coaching, psychology, and business	

Step 4: Look for overlaps and gaps between current and future career

Current career

Before you compare both careers, think of all the elements you wrote down for your future career. Now write down all your current activities and responsibilities. Then break it down into talents and skills, experience, and knowledge.

My current activities:

_____

_____

My talents used to perform these activities:

_____

_____

My skills used to perform these activities:

_____

_____

My experience used to perform these activities:

_____

_____

My knowledge used to perform these activities:

_____

_____

Overlaps

Here you need to find common ground. What are the elements that both career paths share? Are there any? I am sure there are some.

If you look at my two jobs (auditor and coach), at first glance you would say that they are complete opposites, but if you look more closely at the elements of each, you'll see that, as a coach, I use a lot of the talents and skills that I used as an auditor. What differentiates the jobs, among other things, is the end goal and the focus. The goal of my job as an auditor was to improve the functioning of the processes, departments and — ultimately — organizations so that they could generate more money for the shareholders in the most efficient, effective and risk-free way. The basic goal of my job as a coach is to help people to improve in the areas they desire to improve in, so that they can lead a happier life, both privately and professionally.

However, in both jobs I did a lot of talking to people, asking thousands of questions and actively listening to their answers. So in terms of talents and skills, there are a lot of common areas.

Gaps

Now it's time to find your gaps. If you are changing the type of job but staying in the same industry, the biggest gaps will most likely be in talents or skills, and, to some extent, in experience. If you are going for the same type of job, but in a different industry, your biggest gap will be in the area of experience. And if you are making a complete change, generally the biggest gap will be in knowledge — as in my case.

When I decided to make a change and applied for coaching and counseling studies, I had to work really hard during the intake meeting to convince the admission board to accept me. Besides the fact that I would be studying in Dutch rather than in my mother tongue, I had not completed any related studies like psychology or sociology. So from their perspective, the gap was huge. They were really worried that my profile was too far from that of their ideal student, and that I would struggle. Most of the other applicants had a psychology, HR or communication background, but I was Ms. Auditor who had just recently learned to speak Dutch.

I managed to convince them, though. I think my determination and passion for the topic did the trick. In the end, I turned out to be one of the best students in the group! Later we joked about it, as my study coordinator confessed that I had almost been rejected.

Below you see a table in which I have summed up my overlaps and gaps per area. The blank table is for you to fill in.

Dorota's overlaps and gaps.

AREA	OVERLAPS	GAPS
Talents	Empathy Influencing Convincing Synthesizing Learning Writing Achieving	Intuiting Entrepreneurship
Skills	Communicating Questioning Listening Language skills Giving feedback	Motivating Supporting Selling

AREA	OVERLAPS	GAPS
Experience	Business experience Working closely with people from different cultures and backgrounds	Coaching Training Mentoring
Knowledge		Coaching education Various short courses related to communication, coaching, psychology and business

My overlaps and gaps.

AREA	OVERLAPS	GAPS
Talents		
Skills		
Experience		
Knowledge		

Step 5. Answer the following questions

1. What studies or courses do I need to complete in order to start working in this field?

    _____

    _____

2. Time frame — how much time would it take before I could start working in this career? Would it be a couple of weeks, months or years?

    _____

    _____

3. What experience do I need to gain? If, for example, you want to start a shoe shop, it would be handy to have retail experience.

    _____

    _____

4. What talents/skills do I need to develop? If for example you want to become a manager or director, you do need leadership skills.

    _____

    _____

5. What old beliefs about yourself do you need to let go of, and what new beliefs do you need to develop to flourish in this career path? This is often what stops us from getting what we want.

    _____

    _____

6. What values are supported through this career choice?
    Consider how this career choice supports your core values. If you value adventure and you are looking into a career in accounting, you could very well exhaust that option after couple of months.

    _____

    _____

Based on the answers above, you can then assess how difficult it would be to choose a certain path. But another very important thing to consider is your level of enthusiasm towards that path. It would be best, of course, if the difficulty is scored as low and enthusiasm as high, but it does not always work this way. Keep away from the careers with which you score low on enthusiasm, unless you want to be reading this book again soon! I know that going for something difficult, even if you are enthusiastic and passionate about it, is a big step but it really is worth it.

Career under consideration	Difficulty to get into from where I am now (L/M/H)	Level of enthusiasm (L/M/H)

How to choose THE career path?

Now that you have investigated all the ins and outs of a possible career change, the time has come to make a decision. If you have a couple of options in mind, you need to choose one to start with. If you have one option that entails taking a huge step, you might need to make a decision about quitting your current job.

Below I describe different scenarios.

You have a couple of options in mind

How do you narrow down the choices? Above, I gave you a couple of handy tools to help you to make up your mind. It would be easiest to choose a job that is least difficult for you and for which you have the highest level of enthusiasm.

When I was thinking of making my career change, one of the options I considered was to work as an auditor for an NGO or an organization such as the UN. Getting into the UN was definitely not an easy solution; I would rate the level of difficulty as high. However, my enthusiasm was medium. So I went for the option that had a high level of difficulty — coaching — but for which I also had the highest level of enthusiasm.

You have one option in mind

You might already know what it is that you want to be doing but you might have to quit your current job to pursue it. The bigger the gap between your current career path and the future one, the more difficult it can be to go for it.

There are a couple of options here:
  » Start your own company
  » Freelance
  » Work in the same company, industry, or organization but in a different role
  » Work in the same role but in the different company, industry, or organization
  » Work in a different role in the different company, industry, or organization.

Whatever the appropriate option, you need to prepare yourself well for it. If you do not do the necessary preparation, this will allow your inner critic to sabotage your idea.

How to transition?

So you know the career direction you want to go in. Now you need answers to the following questions so you know what kind of plan to put in place to actually make the transition.

Do I need to complete any studies, courses or internships?

Be aware that you will definitely need to complete a new area of studies or a course for certain jobs, but not for all. Many of my clients assume that they will have to complete a lengthy course, so they decide not to start. As I have already mentioned so many times, I suggest that you talk to people who are either in the job you aspire, to or who are hiring for this position. You might think that you need a degree in literature to become a writer, when it might very well not be the case. So before you begin a long and costly process, you need to get out there and talk to those who already have the experience. Do not make assumptions; do a reality check.

The longer I work as a coach, the more I feel that I am not just a coach but a "connector". I have connected so many of my clients either with former or current clients, or people in my extensive network, and I am starting to realize that bringing people together is also a very important part of my job. Many people spend too much time at home drawing up huge plans without ever talking to others to check whether their plans are at all feasible. So whatever plans you have, **stop reading for a moment and email someone who might be able to answer your questions** about your future career and help you to get in touch with an expert in that field.

Done that? Okay, great! Congratulations on taking another step towards your dream career.

How long will it take me to get there?

This is a very important question as it can also determine your other steps. When I decided to quit my job, the first thing I wanted to do was to stay at home with my newborn daughter for at least a year. I knew my husband and I needed enough savings to compensate for my lack of earnings during that year. So even before I fell pregnant, we started saving to allow me to spend time with our daughter without stressing ourselves out.

Later, when I decided to go into coaching, I knew that from the moment of starting my studies it would take a year and a half to start my company — one year of study plus six months to launch my business.

As my initial idea of studying psychotherapy would take five years, I decided to start with a year-long course in coaching and counseling. After that year, if I decided to continue with psychotherapy, I would be able to go straight into second year so either way, the initial course would not be a waste of time. As I have already shared with you, I thought I wanted to change careers to psychotherapy, specializing in childhood trauma, but when I started my coaching studies I realized that I wanted to work with women rather than with children, and that I enjoyed coaching more than I would enjoy being a therapist. But if I had not started this journey, I would still be an auditor who dreamed of becoming a child therapist.

I tell many of my clients that you can prepare all you like, but you cannot account for every possible outcome. You just need to take that first step in your journey.

Does my partner support my decision?

I discuss getting external support for a career move extensively in the following chapter, but my input in the meantime is that if you live together, it is important to include your partner in the decision from the start. The reactions of the partners of my clients vary. Some partners are extremely supportive, pushing my clients to go for their dreams and supporting them in their decisions. If you have partner like that, be grateful! I have also come across many clients whose partners are either neutral or, in the worst cases, completely opposed to their plans. It could be quite a challenge to realize your plan without their support. If you have not yet discussed your career plans with your partner, do it right now.

Do I have enough savings?

Of course we cannot forget about our finances. We still need to pay our bills.

As you know, I planned to spend at least a year at home with my first child. But we had just bought a new apartment and it came with a higher mortgage. To avoid the stress of having to give up the apartment, we decided to start saving ahead of time.

Consider whether your career change will affect you financially — especially if it worsens your situation. If you are planning to stay in the same job, just in a different industry, this might not be the case. But if, like many of my clients, you plan to freelance or start your own company, your earnings may well decrease, at least initially. You need to ask yourself the following critical questions. If you live with your partner, it is best to involve him/her in the thinking and decision-making process.

What is my current financial situation?
>   » How much do I earn per month?
>   » How much do I spend? What are my fixed costs (i.e. mortgage, insurance, car repayments) every month?
>   » How much do I spend on basics like food per month?
>   » How much do I spend on luxuries like going out with my friends?
>   » How much do I save every month?
>   » What is the minimum income I require per month?
>   » Does my future career plan mean that I will earn more, less, or the same in the first few months after the transition?

If it is less:
>   » How much would I earn?
>   » Is it enough to cover the minimum income I require?
>   Yes / No

» Do I need to invest any money towards studies for my future career or setting up my own company? If yes, how much?
Yes / No   Amount
» Do I have any savings that I can use during the transition period? And for how long — three months, six months, a year?
Yes / No   Number of months
» How long do I think it will take me to earn my minimum required income?
» Can I count on the financial support of my partner or family?
Yes / No

Based on the answers above, come up with a plan. For example, one of my clients lives alone and cannot count on the support of others, so it will take her longer to save enough to be able to quit her job and start her own company. If, like my client, you also need to complete new studies, you need to take the duration of the course and the fees into account. My client has remained in her current position while saving and studying.

Another client who wanted to start on his own already had some savings plus his partner had a good job. But he needed to convince his partner that they would have enough money if he had no income for the first year after quitting his job. After fully understanding his plan (financially and career-wise), his partner agreed to it. So my client was able to begin his new career path immediately.

My choice
Based on all the input and the analyzed data, it is time now to make a decision.

The career path that I am choosing is

_____

_____

_____

Clients' Stories

Anna

"Rejecting a job offer in my previous industry was one of the most uncomfortable conversations I have ever had. But because I didn't take the easy option, it ultimately felt like a victory. I needed to close (even lock!) the door to my old life to truly open the door to my new one."

I was born and raised in a small, gray city in post-communist Poland. When I was growing up, I felt that "getting out" was the best way to "make it" in life. Like many other Polish people of my generation, after finishing high school, I left Poland to work as an au pair in the Netherlands. I studied Spanish Language and Culture and I hold a Master's degree in Intercultural Communication. Studies, work, love and curiosity led me to live in Guatemala, Mexico, Denmark, Thailand and, most recently, Switzerland.

Work-wise, I have always been lucky, with interesting opportunities coming my way. I ended up working in sales at an international shoe company and I felt happy with how my life was shaping up. The international assignments, high level of responsibility, lovely people around me, and the feeling of being a part of a family kept me motivated for a very long time. I was valued, I was challenged, and I was progressing quickly. So when I became aware of a nagging voice suggesting that although I was on a fast career track, it was the wrong one, I managed to silence it for another year. I was doing well in sales but I started to wonder if this was what I was meant to do in life. At one point, for want of a better idea and in the hope that a breath of a fresh air would make me happy again, I decided to change companies. This kind of logic seems absurd to me now, but I was confused, and I backed the decision with many rational arguments that enabled me to ignore the real issue. It also felt good to be doing something, rather than not acting at all. I took the new job and couldn't have been happier... for a few months.

The role was challenging, the product helped people to live a healthier life, my colleagues were fun, it was close to my home, and I was happy with what I was earning. Unfortunately, my initial enthusiasm soon wore off. My day-to-day work was about selling and bringing in new customers but closing each new deal gave me only a very brief feeling of accomplishment. At the same time, I was involved with a female networking group called "Lean In". It's a community of women who support each other and grow together through knowledge exchange and peer support. Co-organizing events and seeing the impact they had on the participants made me incredibly enthusiastic and energized. I longed for this feeling, not just occasionally in my spare time, but also at work.

Have you been there, where you feel you have nothing to complain about but for some reason you still feel unsatisfied? To make things worse, you start to blame yourself for being spoiled and ungrateful for all the good things in your life, so you talk yourself into looking at the positives and decide to stop whining? A few weeks in, you're down again and wonder what's wrong with you.

Paradoxically, my wake-up call was an offer to take on a slightly different role within the company. Although I would be able to use more of my core strengths in the new role, I felt that saying "yes" would mean a long-term commitment and I wasn't sure I wanted to make it. After few deep conversations with my family and friends over the weekend, I decided not to accept the offer and, to the surprise of many, to leave the company altogether. It might have seemed like a spontaneous, irrational decision but, truth to be told, this was almost two years in the making. I was not leaving a job, I was leaving an entire career track. When I left the company, I had been there for only 11 months and I didn't have a new job lined up. My entire plan consisted of this: "Take a step back, and don't rush into something new for the sake of it; rather figure out what you want to do in life." This clearly wasn't enough.

That is why the day after I resigned from my job, I was on the phone with Dorota, asking her to help me find a new way. We had met more than 10 years ago at a career fair and had chatted for no longer than 10 minutes, but I liked her instantly, and we exchanged contact details. Over the next few years I followed Dorota's business and read her articles on career development and on being an expat. We weren't in contact but when the time came to work with a career coach, I knew it had to be Dorota.

I decided to try coaching because I believe that you can gain a lot of value from being asked the right questions and from being challenged to come up with meaningful answers. In this case, rather than relying on my family and friends, I decided to speak to a professional coach who wouldn't have any assumptions about my abilities or expectations regarding the path I should take. It felt safer to discuss my thoughts with a stranger, because I wouldn't be worried about hurting their feelings or being judged. This was a gift for me; I wanted to be egoistic, fully focused on myself and speak the truth and only the truth without worrying about the way I phrased it.

For me, career coaching has been as much about figuring out what constitutes a meaningful career, as about living up to my newly articulated values in moments of doubt and fear, and learning to become more comfortable with the uncomfortable. It has been hard work. Unlearning the destructive thinking patterns that have been an integral part of your adult years takes a lot of effort, self-reflection and guts. I wanted a career change, but I had no idea of what I could do instead, and it was painful. I felt I wasn't good enough for anything else and I was worried that I wouldn't get a new job elsewhere. Halfway through the coaching, I got a chance to return to my previous industry, in a similar role but at an even higher level. My old system kicked in and I seriously considered taking up the challenge. However, the more of a reality the prospect became, the more my discomfort increased. In the end, I had stomach pains for a week, as I considered all the pros and cons and admitted to myself that I was going to say "no" to this apparently amazing opportunity. I think I was stammering and my voice was shaking while I was rejecting the offer. It was one of the most uncomfortable conversations I have ever had. But what is interesting is that it ultimately felt like a victory because I hadn't taken the easy option. I needed to close (even lock!) the door to my old life to truly open the door to my new one.

Over the course of the coaching, I did many exercises with Dorota but I found it particularly useful to focus on my values (page 81) and talents (page 101). Freedom and fairness stood out, and when articulated, I saw how they had manifested throughout my life. I felt the indignation rising again while telling Dorota about the times that they were violated. As a result of the coaching, I also see how transferrable my experience and skills are, so I feel much more empowered to tackle anything in life. My self-confidence now comes from within, rather than from external validation.

The truly life-changing exercise was the "Parent-Adult-Child Model" (page 229). It brought tears to my eyes. There has never been a lot of play time in my life and I saw how much I had neglected my inner creative child. I decided to change this. I've always worked hard and only now am I learning what "play" actually means for me. I have always enjoyed taking pictures so recently I made time for a photography course and invested in proper equipment. I spend more time with my family and friends too and try to be outdoors more often, although this is still a struggle.

I feel that I have reconnected with my internal compass of values and that I have gained a deep understanding of what makes me happy and what doesn't. This will guide me through the rest of my life. I'm also happy to report that I have found new and exciting job opportunities in line with the new direction I have chosen. Initially, I spent a few months working part-time for two local NGOs. This gave me the opportunity to explore multiple options at the same time — to combine my work life with my interest in photography.

Both NGOs are in the areas of diversity and inclusion. The first focuses on advancing gender equality in business and the other assists entrepreneurs with a migrant or refugee background who want to start their own business or socio-cultural initiative in Switzerland. Although one of the roles was an entry-level position, I was happy to take a step back career-wise to gain experience in a new area. Combining two dynamic roles with my family, volunteering responsibilities and interests has been difficult at times but even though my income was halved, it was a worthwhile journey. I learned a lot about myself and have met fantastic people along the way.

Within a few months, I was promoted to a role that fulfills me in terms of responsibilities and salary level in one of the jobs. The cherry on top is that I work with inspiring and committed people, I have flexible working hours and am often able to work from home. I feel that the work we do serves a bigger purpose and this is incredibly rewarding.

The things I'm working on now feel so much more like "fun" rather than "work" too, and that's exactly what I wanted to achieve through coaching. I hope you will find the strength within yourself too, to lead the life you truly want. Good luck!

Chapter Thirteen

Who really controls your life?

*"The destiny of every human being is decided by
what goes on inside his skull when confronted by
what goes on outside his skull."*
Eric Berne

The Parent Adult Child Model

Transactional Analysis, developed by Eric Berne (a Canadian psychiatrist and psychotherapist), is one of my favorite theories in psychotherapy by far. It provides a framework, not only for individual and group therapy, but also for communication theories, child development theories, self-development and more. Berne published a couple of books on the topic of Transactional Analysis, including the world-renowned *Games People Play*, and *Transactional Analysis in Psychotherapy*.

He introduced the concept of three ego states, Parent, Adult, and Child. In each ego state, we think, feel, and behave in a different, distinct way. According to his theory of transaction, the way we communicate is determined by our dominant ego state.

So how do you decode it? The Parent ego state relates to the situations where you think, feel, and behave the way you were taught to by your parents. It is the part of your upbringing that relates to behavioral norms, and consists of all the commands and orders we received from our parents. When we are in our Parent ego state we say things like, "Don't talk to strangers," "Put a hat on or you will freeze your ears off," and "You should always be polite to your elders."

The opposite, the Child ego state, mainly relates to the emotions you felt as a young child in certain situations, like happiness, fear, or anger. When we revert to our Child ego state now, we behave in the way we behaved when we were young, without even realizing it.

The Adult ego state relates to the ways we think, feel and act "using all the resources available to [us] as a grown-up[4]." This ego state is aware of its strengths and weaknesses.

In their great book, *TA Today: A New Introduction to Transactional Analysis*, Ian Stewart and Vann Joines added to the Parent Adult Child concept. They split the Parent, Adult, and Child ego states into Nurturing Parent, Controlling Parent, Adult, Free Child, and Adaptive Child.

The **Nurturing Parent** (NP) is the caring part of the parent. It is concerned with the child's wellbeing and often may appear as a mother figure (though men can play this role too). They seek to keep the Child contented, offering a safe haven and unconditional love to calm the Child's troubles. The main role of the NP is to protect and keep the child safe. We develop this ego state through observing our parents and others who took part in our upbringing. When you observe yourself in your daily life, you can easily spot when you are in your NP. It does not necessarily have to be towards your children. You can also act as a Caring Parent towards your partner, friends, colleagues, but also towards yourself.

The language of the NP is characterized by phrases like, "Be careful!", "Be safe", "Take care!" When taken to an extreme it can become suffocating for others. If you do too much of a good job as an NP, you are not giving others the chance to come up with the solutions to their own problems. You are overprotective. The negative consequence of

---

4   TA Today, Page 4

being too much of an NP towards yourself is that you always play it safe, never taking any risks in order to achieve results. I often see it with my clients: they want to change their career, but at the same time they do not want to take the risks that are inherent to change.

However, being a positive NP towards oneself is a blessing. You know where your limits lie, you know when you need to relax, you know how to love and respect yourself. I have also noticed that as women, we are especially good at being a great Nurturing Parent towards others but not towards ourselves.

The **Controlling (or Critical) Parent** (CP) tries to make the Child do as he or she wants them to do, transferring values or beliefs or helping the Child to understand and function in society. The CP is very much about imposing rules and instructions. It is easy to recognize the CP in the language used.

The favorite statements of the CP are, "You should," "You must," "You have to," "You cannot." All that is forbidden comes from the CP. The CP can have a significant negative impact on our lives. First, as a consequence of our own parents being overly critical towards us, it becomes our own inner critic. Judgmental statements such as, "You are stupid" and "You will never make it, don't even try" come from the CP. It is also very often the hidden driving force behind many people's success. It is the slave driver in us that tells us to reach further and aim higher, no matter the sacrifice and no matter what we really want.

The difference between CP and Adult in this case is significant. Both can drive us towards success, but in very different ways. The motivation of the CP is mean and is expressed in the negative self-chatter, "You are not good enough unless you achieve this or that." The Adult part wants us to realize our full potential but without the negative self-talk and with positive support — "Yes, you can do it!"

The **Adult** in us is the "grown up," rational person who talks reasonably and assertively, neither trying to control others nor reacting aggressively towards them. The Adult is comfortable with itself and is, for many of us, our "ideal self" to strive for. For me, the pure manifestation of the Adult is expressed in positive actions. And positive actions start with positive thoughts, which stem from positive self-talk: "I deserve it, I am okay, I am good, I am lovable, I am good enough, I am unique, I can, I want and I DO!"

Very often, at the end of a session I ask my clients, "So what are your next steps?" They usually answer, "I have to start networking" or "I should change my behavior." I then say, "You do not *have* to" or "You *should* not do anything." Using the words "have to" and "should" comes from your Critical Parent ego state. You impose it on yourself, which means the likelihood that you will actually carry through on the action is lower. Formulate the same action but use the language of the Adult: "I want to start networking as it will increase my chances of getting the job I am aiming for, so I will call Mrs. XYZ tomorrow to set up a meeting." This is the Adult talking, and this is when you are really taking responsibility for your actions and your life. This is when things actually happen. If you take nothing else from this book, please remember this part.

If you observe children, you will know immediately when they are in their **Free Child** (FC) state. They like playing and are open, vulnerable, and creative. Free of concern for what others think of them. Free to experiment, free to feel. When they are angry, they scream; when they are happy, they laugh; when they are sad, they cry. When I watch my daughters, I am always amazed at how quickly they switch emotional states. Unlike adults, they do not "hang" in their anger or sadness. One minute they cry, the other, they laugh. That is the beauty of the Free Child — total freedom.

In our grown-up lives, we also act from our FC ego state at times — when we are creative, when we dream, when we act without thinking of the consequences, when we play sport, when we love.

Being in our FC also means being egoistic and egocentric, it is me, me, me and my, my, my. I want this and I want it now. Being in the FC is for some the ultimate definition of happiness, but as it is so self-centered, it can be perceived as a negative behavior. As with all ego states, it has its positive and negative sides.

When working with my clients, I often notice that unhappiness and dissatisfaction in both their personal and professional lives come from not spending enough time in this ego state.

The **Adaptive Child** (AC) reacts to the world around them, either changing themselves to fit in or rebelling against the forces they feel. The core concept of the AC is that you adapt your behavior in order to follow the instructions of someone else's Parent ego state.

Think of situations when you were a child and your mom asked you to do something you didn't like doing. In my case, that was eating porridge. The options were: conform to the rule or rebel against it. Both were the answer to something that was imposed. I had limited "free" choice in the situation, so I was in my AC. Think of the situations when you did something to get the attention of your parents. It could have been a good or bad thing — either way, you just wanted them to notice you. In this case you were also acting from your AC.

In our grown-up life we all act from this ego state — some of us from time to time, others quite often. How do you know when you are acting from your Adaptive Child?

When you feel that you do things that are not in line with what YOU want. When you adapt your behavior to please others whether it is your partner, parent, child, colleague, or friend. It occurs when you are pleasing, rebelling, or adapting your behavior to someone else's demand or instruction.

Acting from AC can have both positive and negative aspects. When you are a part of a team and you need to adapt your way of thinking so that the team will win, it is a positive application of the AC ego state. But when you feel that you are betraying yourself to please someone else, it is a negative application.

Ego states and career choices

In every moment of our lives, we find ourselves in one of these ego states, irrespective of whether we are alone or in company. Our ego states often depend on the people we are dealing with or the situations we are in.

We can also consider what different ego states have to say about our career choices.

Our **Critical Parent**, which often uses the same arguments as our parents used and/or still do, usually pushes us for success in the eyes of others. People who listen to the CP state most of the time are often successful in society, holding senior positions. But for their CP, it is never good enough; this ego state wants others to see us as successful, irrespective of what we want ourselves. The Critical Parent uses expressions like, "I should," "I am supposed to" and "I must." The CP is also most likely to give you very rational, "realistic" career advice with little space for your dreams and ideals. When I talk to my clients about this, I often hear them say, "My CP wants me to grow further in the career path that I already have." The Critical Parent is also the one that thinks you should spend a lot of your time on improving your weaknesses so that you can become Mr./Ms. Perfect.

When I was considering my own career switch, my CP was screaming, "It is not realistic," "You have already spent so much time and money on your current career path" and "You should not disappoint others."

On the other hand, the **Nurturing Parent** wants to save us from taking too much risk in our lives in general and also in our career. This ego state will most likely try to convince you to stay in your current job. "It is not so bad after all," it says. It tells you that you need to be happy with what you already have and not to demand too much. All to keep you safe! Far from risk but also far from being fully alive. The NP uses expressions such as, "Be careful" and "It is dangerous." As the NP also wants you to be happy, it comes up with ideas that could make you happy, but that are quite safe.

While I was considering my career change, one of my ideas was to continue as an auditor but in an organization that was doing something good for the world. I now realize that this was the perfect choice for the Nurturing Parent. It was giving me a bit of what I wanted, but not too much.

The **Free Child** wants one thing: to be free! This is often where the key to our happiness lies. Free Child can sound like this: "I want to be rich and live in the Bahamas," "I want to have an adventurous life" or "I want to quit my job and help save the Amazon rain forest." This voice is often drowned out by the Critical or Nurturing Parent saying that it is irresponsible, not realistic and so on.

My **Free Child** wanted me to become a psychotherapist. It was my crazy dream. I remember reading tons of books on psychology and self-help. I also remember reading Irvin D. Yalom's novel about a psychotherapist, *Lying on the Couch*, and I thought, "Why can't I have that job?" Finally, in combination with my Adult, I took the decision to follow the FC dream.

The **Adaptive Child** wants to please everyone and listens closely to what other Critical and Nurturing Parents have to say about their life and career. This can be divided into two further ego states: one that changes his/her behavior to please others and the other that rebels. The Adaptive Child differs from the Free Child in that it always reacts in relation to others. It always wants to be noticed.

If the obedient **Adaptive Child** is your dominant ego state, it requires you to choose a job that pleases others. The rebellious child chooses just the opposite. The problem here is that it does not take your own needs into consideration. A couple of my clients chose their profession just to show their parents that they would not obey them.

Last but not least, we want to know what our **Adult** ego state has to say. In this state, we are aware of our strengths and weaknesses, and feel comfortable with ourselves. If we want to be fulfilled in our career, the Adult needs to listen to all the parts and make a decision. I would say that a partnership between Free Child and Adult is the best recipe for a meaningful career and happy life in general, but input from all ego states is necessary.

When I started taking my dream of becoming a psychotherapist seriously, one thing that bothered me was the time frame. Studying psychotherapy takes five years. All the other ego states had something to say about it — things like: "What if you do not like it?" and "It is such a big investment of time and money." I remember having a good chat about it with my husband. As I mentioned before, I decided to start with a year-long course in coaching and counseling. After that, I could either finish with a diploma in coaching and counseling and start my practice, or continue with the second year of psychotherapy. This sounded like a great plan. It was a plan made by my Adult, but the first input came from the Free Child.

Exercise: What advice do my ego states give me about my career?

Think about all your career options. What do your ego states say about them? What do they advise you? What other voices (of your friends, parents, partner) do you hear through them?

My Critical Parent wants me to do/become:

_____

_____

My Nurturing Parent wants me to do/become:

_____

_____

My Free Child wants me to do/become:

_____

_____

My Adaptive Child wants me to do/become:

_____

_____

My Adult chooses to:

_____

_____

Chapter Fourteen

Empowering and Limiting Beliefs

*"Those who cannot change their minds
cannot change anything."*
George Bernard Shaw

Limiting Beliefs

The truth is, all dreams begin and end with mindset. Ultimately, it is what you believe is possible or not that steers you towards changing your career in the right direction or not. I often see it in my clients. They have great ideas for their career path, but whether they actually bring their ideas to life very much depends on what they think and believe about themselves and the idea. As Dr. Carol S. Dweck, a psychology professor, wrote in *Mindset*, "The view you adopt for yourself profoundly affects the way you lead your life."

According to Dr. Dweck, we can develop a fixed or a growth mindset. Once you have a fixed mindset, you believe that you are born with a certain set of skills and talents, that are unchangeable. If, on the contrary, you have a growth mindset, you believe that you can grow and develop yourself, your talents and skills.

We develop strategies to cope with what our parents and other relevant people tell us about ourselves. For example, if we are always praised for being cheerful we become more cheerful than if this attribute had not been emphasized.

Our mindset also stems from what we were taught to believe about the world and ourselves. Our thoughts and beliefs influence how we feel, feelings influence our actions, and actions influence our lives.

We are often unaware of our own beliefs. It is also true that by holding those beliefs we can limit ourselves.

In the past, I really liked the saying, "The sky IS the limit." Then I heard a variation, "The sky is NOT the limit." Do you see how I was imposing a limit on myself in the first one? I was saying, "To here and no further." Even if "there" was very far away, it was limited. By adopting the second version, I shifted my thinking to, "I will see where I get to, as long as I keep challenging myself."

So how are beliefs formed? Through repetition of what we hear and are told about the world, others and ourselves. If you were often told, "You are a sweet girl," when you were young, then one of your core beliefs about yourself will be "I am a sweet girl, and sweet girls do not ..." A common core belief is "Work hard and you will be rewarded." Also, "The new or unknown is dangerous."

Often what we believe has little to do with reality. But it will form your reality nonetheless. So you will achieve as much in your life as you allow yourself to.

There are different types of beliefs.

Beliefs about who you are

As mentioned, these beliefs are based on what you heard about yourself, and on various experiences in your early life and how you coped with them. They are also based on the nature of your interactions with your parents, siblings, and others.

I grew up with the conviction that I am highly rational. The origin of this belief was partly in the difference in character between my younger sister and me. She was quite emotional, while I did not show my emotions and was much more introverted and quiet. So there was a polarity: me, quiet and rational; my sister, lively and emotional. I strengthened this early belief by thinking and talking about myself as a rational person. It was only fairly recently, in conversation with a friend, that I realized that I am not so sure whether I really am all that rational. I realized that I am also quite emotional and intuitive in my own way. However, I never allowed myself to show this part of my personality, as I decided early on that I am rational and rejected all the thoughts, actions, and feelings of someone less rational.

This is a result of the fact that we have a strong need for consistency. We need our behavior to be in line with our thoughts, beliefs, and values. So if you believe you are rational, you will act rationally and any attempt to act emotionally will give you an unpleasant feeling of dissonance.

Without being aware of it, I took many mental short cuts in my thinking and came up with recipes for how I should or shouldn't act.

I am rational therefore I do not cry.
I am rational therefore I am not very creative.
I am rational therefore I am not overly emotional.
I am rational therefore I am not intuitive.

When I was deciding to change my career, it was internally a tough decision to take due to my belief that "I am rational, therefore I take rational and realistic actions." In the opinion of my rational self, it was frivolous to follow my dream. I often fight my rational self. But now I am aware that it just comes from the belief I built when I was a child and I can build another belief about myself, which is "I am a dreamer and I act on my dreams." If I had not started to believe this, I would never have written this book.

Our beliefs about who we are can be quite difficult to change as they form the core of our identity. If we start to shake this "tree" of beliefs, it can leave us feeling chaotic and lost. So please always seek professional help when dealing with these issues and when you feel you could become emotionally unstable. Always take good care of yourself.

What are your beliefs about who you are?

Finish the following statements. Write as many beliefs about yourself as you can.

I am _____ I am not _____
I am _____ I am not _____
I am _____ I am not _____

Beliefs about what you can or cannot do

These beliefs do not go as deeply into our core identity as the beliefs about who you are. They are also formed by what you were taught to believe about yourself, but are also based on your capacity to deal with different situations.

Beliefs such as "I listen well," "I am good at taking care of others," "I am bad at math," "I cannot write" or "I am not good at creating things" express what you believe you can and cannot do. I do not mean that they are all untrue and that you should fight all your beliefs. But I do say that you should examine carefully what you were taught to believe about yourself.

For as long as I can remember, I also believed "I am not a creative person" and "I am not good at creating things." Did I start believing this because I was not really good at drawing, singing or acting? This could well be the case. But this belief spread to other parts of my life. Then one day my husband said, "You are really good at creating new things for your business." And I agreed, because I love to invent and create new programs, blogs and ideas for my business. So the belief "I am not creative" is simply not true.

This is the danger of our beliefs: they spread to various other aspects of our lives.

What are your beliefs about what you can and cannot do?

Finish the following statements. Write as many beliefs about yourself as you can.

I can _____ I can't _____
I can _____ I can't _____
I can _____ I can't _____

Beliefs about the outside world

We all use these beliefs to simplify our perception of the world. They relate to aspects of life such as love, work, money, family, communication, and many more.

Examples of the most common widely spread beliefs are:

You need to work hard to become rich.
Money stinks.
No pain, no gain.
Life ends after 50.
Love hurts.
People are not to be trusted.

The problem with these beliefs is that we treat them as absolute truths. Once we do that, we limit our perception of reality, which is, in fact, more nuanced. For each of these types of beliefs, there is probably an example that proves just the opposite.

We choose to hold certain beliefs. Take the belief, "Love hurts." This is based on the experience of heartbreak in our youth. We decide that love does indeed hurt, then extrapolate this belief to the future: when we fall in love again, we will be hurt. To avoid potential pain, we cut off our feelings.

We inherit some of these beliefs from our parents, either because we hear them expressed verbally, or because we see them acting in a certain way. My parents worked very hard, and my dad in particular worked hard physically to earn a good living for us. One of my core beliefs about money is "You need to work really hard to become wealthy." So whenever I achieve something without much effort, it feels less worthwhile.

It is important to recognize what you believe and choose to believe, as these beliefs rather than reality shape the quality of our lives. So if you believe "I can conquer the world," the chances of doing this are much higher than if you believe "I am a loser and life is painful."

I love to use metaphors, and this one is useful: Beliefs are like glasses through which we perceive the world. What do your glasses look like? Are they rosy? Or are they dark?

What are your most common beliefs about the outside world?

Write as many beliefs about your perception of the outside world as you can. Think about items such as: relationships, money, people, health, age, and more.

Exercise: Beliefs and your career path

Now take a moment to think about the vision of your career that you came up with in the previous chapters. What do you want to achieve in the next one, three, and five years?

Think about it as an ideal, rather than approaching it from a rational perspective. This will make it easier to examine the mindset and beliefs you hold onto.

For example, you might say, "In three years' time I want to be a millionaire" or "In five years' time I want to be VP HR of a multinational company" or "Next year I want to transition from being an accountant to becoming a yoga teacher."

My career goal/dream is:

_____

Listen carefully to what is going on in your mind. I am sure you can already hear a voice, whispering or even shouting:

> *It is not realistic.*
> *You are too old.*
> *You have already chosen your career once/twice, now stick to it.*
> *A career is not a hobby; you need to take it seriously.*
> *If everyone had a job that he/she loves, who would do the boring work?*

So please write down your limiting beliefs below. Take a moment to think who taught you those beliefs: your parents, grandparents, teachers, friends.

They taught you this when you were a child because they wanted to protect you, but now that you are a grown woman or man, you can take care of yourself.

Also think about how these beliefs limit you. What would you do if you decided not to hold on to them anymore?

Limiting belief 1

_____

_____

Who taught me this belief?

_____

_____

How does it negatively impact my life and career?

_____

_____

If I stop believing it, then

_____

_____

Limiting belief 2

_____

_____

Who taught me this belief?

_____

_____

How does it negatively impact my life and career?

_____

_____

If I stop believing it, then

_____

_____

Limiting belief 3

_____

_____

Who taught me this belief?

_____

_____

How does it negatively impact my life and career?

_____

_____

If I stop believing it, then

_____

_____

Limiting belief 4

_____

_____

Who taught me this belief?

_____

_____

How does it negatively impact my life and career?

_____

_____

If I stop believing in it, then

_____

_____

Limiting belief 5

_____

_____

Who taught me this belief?

_____

_____

How does it negatively impact my life and career?

_____

_____

If I stop believing it, then

_____

_____

Look fear in the eye

> "Most of us have two lives. The life we live, and the unlived
> life within us. Between the two stands resistance."
> Steven Pressfield, The War of Art

Most negative beliefs are the product of our Parent ego state. As mentioned in the previous chapter, this part of our psyche tries to protect us from taking too much risk. The root of all of these statements is fear. This negative part of the Parent ego state is called the saboteur, as its main job is to sabotage you and your dreams.

One of the best books on this topic is *The War of Art: Break Through the Blocks and Win Your Inner Creative Battles* by Steven Pressfield. He called the inner saboteur who is trying to keep you from the work that you are meant to be doing "Resistance". Resistance, or the saboteur, feeds us fear for breakfast, lunch, and dinner and takes all kinds of forms and shapes. Although it comes from within, it often seeks outside partners to help it to do the job.

Now think about the main fear that your saboteur arouses. For example, I sabotaged myself for months while trying to make a video. Although I really wanted to do this, and I knew it would be very helpful to my clients, I paid careful attention to my saboteur, which fed me thoughts like, "Who are you to tell people what to do?", "Your voice sounds really funny" and many more. Behind all that nonsense, there was a fear of being judged, of not being accepted by others — the fear of not belonging.

Look at your limiting beliefs. What fears are they the gatekeepers of?

My main fears are:

Fear 1

Fear 2

Fear 3

Eliminating limiting beliefs

What will happen if you keep believing those statements? Where will they lead to in your life and your career?

Your life may be in order, but is it a bit too safe and boring? Do you want it? Or do you (secretly) want something else? If the answer to the last question is, "Yes, I want something else," then please read the following section carefully.

The thing about fear is that it will not go away anytime soon. So you have to find ways to manage your fears.

For each fear, answer these questions and write down the answers:

Fear 1

How realistic is this fear?

What is the worst-case scenario?

How could I deal with it?

Fear 2

How realistic is this fear?

What is the worst-case scenario?

How could I deal with it?

Fear 3

How realistic is this fear?

What is the worst-case scenario?

How could I deal with it?

Now look at your fears again. Do they seem less scary?

Dealing with excuses

So you have finally figured out what it is that you want to do next in your career. Now the problems start. You need to change. But from the moment you reach a decision, your brain becomes very creative, providing all sorts of excuses for not making the change and staying where you are instead. Do not be misled. As you have learned previously, this is either the voice of your Critical Parent or Adaptive Child. If they shout loudly enough, they will scare you and talk you out of your plan for change. I have seen it happen.

What is the difference between an excuse and an obstacle? I define an excuse as *a conscious or unconscious thought that puts a stop to your action.* You treat it as a legitimate reason to stop working on your goals. So you say to yourself, "I do not have time to change my career," and before even evaluating the truth of this thought, you give up on the idea of changing or developing your career further. On the other hand, I define an obstacle as something that you are willing to, and can, deal with. Time and money can be obstacles, but the difference is that you do not lose sight of your main goal. You tell yourself, "Okay, so I do not have enough money to start my new studies just yet, but what can I do to save enough to be able to realize my goal?" Do you see the difference? It is not in the problem itself. The issue remains the same, but the fundamental difference is your attitude towards it. In the first case, your attitude comes either from your Parent ego state, which is often critical, or from your helpless Child state, which is a passive victim. In the second case, your attitude is about being in the Adult ego state, being in control, and taking action.

Below is a list of the most common excuses we come up with to avoid change. I didn't stop there; with every excuse there is a remedy. So the excuses are transformed into obstacles you can overcome. Remember that these excuses are in your head, they are not reality, but they can manifest if you do not deal with them properly.

Excuse number 1: I do not have time to change my career.

Busy. Busy. Busy. We are all busy — running around in circles. I often hear my clients say, "I do not have time. I have so many things to do." But usually when we start looking more deeply into the issue of time, it turns out that there is plenty of it. If you get your priorities right and look critically at how you spend your time, you will easily find two to three hours per day! A lot of extra time to spend on your career change or development.

Remedy

The best remedy is to track your activities for a week. In a notebook, write down all the things you do during the day, including the timing. After a week, look critically at how you spend your time. You might find that you spend up to a couple of hours a day on Facebook, email, phone, Internet, or TV. Of course we all need time to relax, but ask yourself if you really cannot dedicate one or two hours a day to something you really care about: the development of your professional life. In the end, the time you spend on social media or on watching TV will not add significantly to your happiness, but spending time on yourself and your career will! Choose your priorities and choose them wisely!

This is one of my excuses

Y ( )   N ( )

How do I plan to deal with it?

_____

Excuse number 2: I cannot afford the career change.

Some careers require more investment than others. This is a fact; there's nothing we can do to change it. If you want to become a broker or a real estate agent, you need to complete certain studies that require money.

So what do you do if you have discovered that you do not have enough money to start a new path now? You need to plan how you will come up with additional money — nothing illegal, though!

Remedy
Read the Chapter Twelve "Transition Plan", which includes tips on how to come up with additional savings to realize your plan.

This is one of my excuses
Y ( )　　　N ( )

How do I plan to deal with it?

Excuse number 3: What will my parents, partner, children, or anyone else say about my change?

I wrote elaborately on getting support from the people around you in Chapter Fifteen. It is one of the most crucial elements to your success, so please do not treat it lightly. As you read earlier, according to US psychologist Abraham Maslow, one of our basic needs is for love, acceptance and belonging. We need others not only in order to survive, but also to live a happy and fulfilled life. That is why one of our primary fears is the fear of not being accepted. We do crazy things to be accepted, we often change our opinion to please others, and we are paralyzed if we have to give a brief speech in public.

No wonder we worry about what those closest to us will say about our career change. What they think is important to you. My husband's thoughts on my new business projects are important to me and I often consult him. So don't get me wrong, you do need to talk to your partner about your career plans. However, we sometimes take the opinion of others more seriously than our own. And that is when things can go wrong.

Remedy

First identify whose approval you are actually seeking. Is it that of your partner? Or is it the approval of your parents, sister, brother, best friend? Sometimes I even hear from my clients that they feel that it is "society" that does not grant them the approval to move forward.

So if this is the excuse you keep giving yourself, take a moment now to think about whose opinion you fear most.

Fill in the following sentences:

I fear the opinion of my _____

I am afraid that my _____ will not approve of my new career idea.

Once you have identified whose disapproval you fear, you cannot know for sure whether this is valid unless you have heard it directly from the given person. If it is your partner's opinion that you are worried about, read the Chapter Fifteen "Getting Support" and talk to your partner.

If the opinion that you are so afraid of is of your parents, or other family members or friends of the older generation, you need to acknowledge that you are an adult, not a child any longer. This is sometimes particularly difficult when our parents are involved. After all, they will always be our parents and we, their children. But they do not and should not have the same power over us as they had when we were kids. Those times are gone. If you had parents who were very strict and were often in the role of the Critical Parent, you might actually still be afraid of what they will think and say. But you cannot live your life pleasing your parents.

Your life is your own. You are responsible for making the best of it. If you are living your life based on the expectations of others, you are living their life. Taking responsibility can be difficult. It means that you might make mistakes and there will be no one else to blame but yourself. This is often why we choose to stick with the excuse, "What will others say?" But do you want to live your life like that? Do you want to experience regret over the things you haven't done when you reach 80 or 90 years old? I am sure you don't. So go ahead and say it out loud:

I take responsibility for my own life and I make my own decisions.

This is one of my excuses
Y ( )   N ( )

How do I plan to deal with it?

_____

Excuse number 4: What if I fail?

This is one of the most common reasons that people stay stuck for years or sometimes even a lifetime. What if I fail? And even worse, what if others see that I have failed? This excuse is based on the fear of making a huge, irreversible mistake as a result of changing. So where does this fear come from? We were taught that mistakes are to be avoided at all costs. Mistakes are bad, dangerous and should be punished. But what if we started perceiving mistakes as a part of the game, and as learning opportunities?

When I started my coaching business, one of my first assignments was a workshop for a well-known multinational company. I was extremely stressed. In addition, it was the first time I would be running a workshop for a large group. The workshop was a disaster. I was not prepared for dealing with so many people. I was so stressed that I didn't even dare to stand in front of the group, I just sat behind the table and murmured things probably no one could hear or understand. Afterwards, I wanted to run away and hide and never hold a workshop again. I felt deeply ashamed and disappointed. Some months later, I was asked to give another workshop. I said yes. Thanks to the experience I had with the previous one, I knew how to prepare. It went much better.

The more workshops I gave, the better I became. Now I give speeches to a couple of hundred people at time. Although quite painful, the first workshop was my biggest learning curve, and I am now very grateful for it.

Remedy

If you are suffering from a fear of failure, think of what you can learn about yourself if you fail. Look fear straight in the eye and answer the following questions:

1. What is the best thing that could happen if I changed or developed my career?

   _____

   _____

2. What is the worst thing that could happen if I changed or developed my career?

   _____

   _____

3. How would I deal with it? How would I find my way out?

   _____

   _____

4. What would I learn from it?

   _____

   _____

5. What is the most likely outcome?

   _____

   _____

6. When did I last feel that I had failed?

   _____

   _____

7. How did I deal with it?

   _____

   _____

8. Final lessons learnt from this experience?

_____

_____

This is one of my excuses

Y ( )   N ( )

How do I plan to deal with it?

_____

Excuse number 5: I have already invested so much time, energy and money in my current career.

If you have been telling yourself this, ask yourself how many more years you want to spend in your current job. Imagine doing that for the rest of your life. How does it feel? Have a look at the "Timeline" exercise (page 64) to remind yourself of it again.

I remember that I thought a lot about this. When I moved to the Netherlands and got a job as an internal auditor, I did not know much about auditing. I did know a lot about finance and business but nothing specifically on risk management and so on. I had to go through additional courses to get up to speed with my colleagues. It meant passing four quite difficult exams. Often, during my travels abroad (approximately half of my total work time), when my colleagues went out for dinner and drinks, I stayed in my room to study for my exams. I spent many hours studying. When I started to think about a career change, one of the things that was stopping me was exactly this: "I have put so much time and effort into auditing, and now I want to stop?!" But then when I asked myself if I could imagine staying in this job and studying further related topics, my answer was: "No!" However painful it was to let go of the old career, I felt I had to change. So I did. And you can do that too!

Remedy

Choosing something new always means saying goodbye to something old. And it is only natural that saying goodbye causes pain. If you accept the pain, and you tell yourself that it is also okay to feel sad about letting go, I am sure it will make your decision easier.

I want to let go of _____

and by doing this I say YES to _____

This is one of my excuses

Y ( )   N ( )

How do I plan to deal with it?

_____

Excuse number 6: I do not have the right education to change my career.

If your new career path is completely different from the current one, it might mean that you will need to complete a new course. I had to do it as an auditor who wanted to become a psychotherapist or coach. I didn't have the theoretical background or credentials for the new job, so I had to start from scratch. As you know, initially I wanted to study psychotherapy but as it was a five-year course, I decided to start with one year of coaching and counseling studies to see if it was the right direction for me. And it was!

Remedy

If your career change requires that you complete studies that entail a long-term commitment (more than a year), I suggest that you first take similar shorter courses to make sure it really is the path for you. Look on www.edx.org and www.coursera.org to see if there are any courses similar to what you have in mind.

Talk to people in the job you want; ask for their input on the education they needed to get there. Acquiring new qualifications is a step on your career path that definitely should not be used as an excuse.

This is one of my excuses
Y ( )   N ( )

How do I plan to deal with it?

_____

Excuse number 7: I am too old. It is too late.

It is never too late. Ask yourself: even if it was just for a month or a year, would you prefer to be in your old job or would you like to follow the new path? I have many clients in their mid-thirties who feel that they are too old for a change.

As you know by now, I also considered myself too old for change and the studies too long, which is why I took a short-cut and did a year of coaching and counseling instead of five years of psychotherapy. And that turned out for the best because I discovered that I am much better suited to and derive greater enjoyment from being a coach than I would have as a therapist.

Remedy
If you also think you are too old, here are some great examples of people who made their mark in their "second" careers.

Raymond Chandler, who was unsuccessful as a journalist and also worked as an executive in an oil company, published his first book at the age of 51. Andrea Bocelli was a lawyer before he decided to dedicate himself fully to singing at 34. Julia Child wrote her first cookbook and became a celebrity chef at the age of 50. Prior to that, she worked in media and advertising. Before starting her career as a fashion designer at age 40, Vera Wang was a figure skater and a journalist. She is one of the top fashion designers for women.

For some jobs, it could be too late, though. If you are 65 and you would like to become a heart surgeon, it might indeed be too late. But in many cases it is not. If you still believe that you are too old, I want you to check the facts; talk to people, find out about admission requirements. I want hard evidence. No assumptions, okay?

Answer honestly:

My age:

_____

What proof do I have that I am too old for the considered career?

_____

This is one of my excuses

Y ( )   N ( )

How do I plan to deal with it?

_____

Excuse number 8: I don't know how to change.

This could actually be one of the reasons you are reading this book, right? It is important to ask yourself the next question: what exactly is it that you do not know? Once you know what you are missing, it will be easier to find out how to make the change.

Remedy

In Chapter Twelve "Transition Plan", you will find detailed and concrete steps you need to take in order to move forward. If you break the process into small steps and take just one step at a time, the career you wish for will become a reality.

You might think you do not know the right people. In this case, read excuse number 9. One thing is for sure, if you do not know how, where or what, you need to ask for help to move on.

This is one of my excuses
Y ( )   N ( )

How do I plan to deal with it?

Excuse number 9: I do not know the right people.

The majority of my international clients moved from abroad to the Netherlands, so obviously their network was rather limited at first.

As mentioned earlier, to change or develop your career, you need help from others. If you think you do not know the right people, you need to plan a way to get to know them. They surely do exist. All you need to do is to find them.

First, identify the people you are looking for. Is it a recruiter who can help you to get a new job? Is it someone who is already doing the job you want? Once you know who you need, you can communicate it much more easily to others. The next thing to do is to identify who you know already.

Remedy
Take a big piece of paper and write down "me" in the middle. Around that, write down the names of people you know who you think might help. Do not be too critical here; rather include too many than too few. You never know who they know! Prioritize your list. Who among those closest to you might know the right people? Take another piece of paper and write down their names. They are your priority contacts, so number this 1. Then make a second list, labeled 2, of those you don't know as well and who you think would be less helpful. The last group is for anyone you haven't had any contact with for years or who has limited

ability to help you. Facebook and your LinkedIn account are great tools for identifying people who can help. Now start contacting them to ask for help. Here are some handy tips on how to do it:

1. Always try to contact them in person first. So if you can visit someone, do that rather than call. If you cannot visit, but you can call, do that rather than sending an email.
2. Be specific about what you are asking for. You need to prepare this. How do you want this person to help you? If you are vague, the risk is that they won't know what to do so they do nothing.
3. Always thank them and ask if you can do something in return
4. Follow up. If you haven't heard anything after two weeks, give them a call. People are busy. They might really want to help but you might not be their number one priority. So don't be shy — call.

This is one of my excuses
Y ( )   N ( )

How do I plan to deal with it?

_____

Excuse number 10: It is too difficult.

This is one of the most common excuses I hear. The statement "It is too difficult" often equates to "I am not going to do that." If it is difficult, you tend to feel that you have a legitimate reason for inaction. But the question is, why should it be easy? If it is easy, then is it worth the effort? I often hear my inner voice saying, "It is too difficult, don't do it, do not even try." I have experienced this particularly while practicing Yin yoga. In this style of yoga, you need to stay in a certain position for several minutes — five, 10, 15 or more. These positions often seem very easy initially. When I first joined the class, we started with the child pose. For the first minute, it was really easy. I thought, "Oh, this is really easy and relaxing." After one more minute, my mind was already drifting. My knees started to ache, my hips were stiff and painful. I felt the blood pulsing in my head. Then I heard the teacher say, "Four more minutes." Four more minutes!!! No, it is too difficult, too hard, too painful. I changed position. After a few more classes, I realized that these simple yoga exercises have a direct link to many other situations in my life; when something begins to feel uncomfortable, I immediately want out, so that I do not feel pain, discomfort or any other unpleasant feeling. After practicing Yin yoga (which now is my favorite style) more often, I have discovered that I can take a breath, relax and give in to the pain and discomfort rather than fight it. What a liberating experience! And I have also realized that I can apply this to other aspects of my life. I discovered that I can go beyond my momentary discomfort, so that I no longer experience it as discomfort.

When dealing with your career change or development, at which point in time did you start telling yourself that it was too difficult, and you need to stop? Take a moment to think about it.

So in which situations do you say to yourself "It is too difficult, I want to stop"? The following pointers will help you to get past it.

Remedy
1. Change the label from negative to positive — from "It is too difficult = it is going to be painful => so I am not going to do that" to "It is difficult = it is going to be a new learning experience => let's go for it."
2. Be aware that your brain plays tricks on you. I have already talked extensively about it in this chapter when describing fear and limiting beliefs.
3. Be aware of your patterns. Analyze situations when you stop working on your long-term goals and go after short-term pleasure instead. (Procrastination is its other name!)
4. Take charge of your life by tackling small (unpleasant) steps first and making sure you do them.

5. Treat yourself to something fancy once you have completed a difficult or painful task. This way, you will still enjoy short-term pleasures — but ones that will not deflect you from working on your long-term goals.
6. Practice positive thoughts. This will lead to positive beliefs and, in turn, to positive habits.
7. Ask yourself daily: "What have I done today to get me closer to my ultimate goal?"
8. Forgive yourself if you haven't done anything that day. But start again the next day!
9. Surround yourself with positive people who are also aiming for their own big goals. Ask them for support if you are going off track.

This is one of my excuses
Y ( )　　　N ( )

How do I plan to deal with it?

_____

Excuse number 11: I am not quite ready yet for the change — maybe next year...

Yes, of course, maybe next year, maybe in two years' time — maybe never. Your brain is playing tricks on you, so that you delay the decision-making process, as its main goal is to keep you safe. You have to realize that the circumstances will never be right or perfect and, in fact, they do not need to be. However, it's a different story if you have made a concrete plan to change your job or career in, say, a year's time because you need to save money or complete a new course.

Remedy
Ask yourself what it is that you are scared of. Very often, behind this excuse lies a deeper one. You need to take care of the deeper one first,

otherwise it will sabotage all your efforts. Check the section on fears again. What I am really scared of is

---

This is one of my excuses
Y ( )   N ( )

How do I plan to deal with it?

Excuse number 12: If I quit my job and go for my dream, who will do the boring work? We can't all have what we want.

Well, if you change your career it won't be you! Maybe this sounds a bit harsh, and my intention is not to offend, but I think this is one of the most disingenuous excuses I have ever heard. Think of the question *"Who will do the boring work?"* in a different way. Why would you not want to benefit others by doing the job that you love, that you are good at and that has a positive effect on society? By staying stuck in your "boring" job, you are not doing anyone any good, are you? Who is benefiting from the fact that you feel stuck in your career? No one! Not you, not your family, and not the millions of poor people who really are stuck in their miserable jobs. I know this may hit a nerve, but I just want you to wake up! The world needs people who want to share their talents and who are passionate about what they do.

Remedy
Make a shift from whiner to winner! When I asked my clients, friends, and people I know what they would like to read about in my book, most of them said, "Inspirational stories of others who have changed their careers for the better." People need to hear positive stories in order to believe that they can do it too. Wouldn't it be wonderful if you were an example that it is possible? How would that make you feel? This is another way in which you can have a positive impact on others.

If you are reading this book, it means that you were born at the right time, in the right country and that you do have control over your own life. Do not waste it!

This is one of my excuses
Y ( )   N ( )

How do I plan to deal with it?

Excuse number 13: In my current job, I am much better off than my family and friends. Am I not spoilt in wanting something else?

Every now and then, I hear this from a client. They feel guilty that they want something else, since others (often family members and close friends) are envious of what they have now. Do you also feel that way? Do you also feel guilty, do you say to yourself: "I am spoilt; I should be happy with what I have, I should not be complaining"?

Remedy
Ask yourself this: "Will your family, friends, or whoever else you are thinking of be worse off once you get a better job, or once you are finally happy with your professional life?" That's the first part.

Next, I would like you to realize that this is a natural process. Once we reach the level in which our basic needs are fulfilled (I discussed Maslow's pyramid of needs in Chapter One), we naturally aspire to the next level. That is just the way we are. You cannot fight with nature. Well, of course you can, but do you want to?

It might well be that you are now ready to reach the highest level of "self-actualization" while your family member or friend might be at the level of "safety" or "belonging". You have different needs at the moment. It is not better or worse, just different.

So please do not feel guilty and do not apologize for your own needs. As long as you are not doing any harm to others, you need to follow your needs just as others need to follow theirs.

Lastly, many of my clients are not happy in their current careers generally for one of two reasons. The first reason is that they do a job that is not in line with their values and talents. The second one is that they do not see the meaning or purpose of what they are doing.

The thing is, with both talents and meaning, once you have found them and the job that combines both, you will certainly thrive as you never have before. And that means that other people around you, the organization you are working at, will benefit. No one benefits from you remaining stuck, feeling miserable, using your weaknesses and, as a consequence, underperforming in your job.

The bottom line is that you should not feel guilty for aiming higher and continuously seeking peak performance by better understanding your talents and finding meaning in your life and career. You deserve to feel special and empowered! In the long term, everyone will benefit from that.

This is one of my excuses
Y ( )   N ( )

How do I plan to deal with it?

Excuse number 14: I can only change once I have completely figured out all the details.

This excuse is a common one for the perfectionists among us. If you feel that whatever you do is never good enough or never quite finished, you might well be a perfectionist too. The thing is, however detailed your plan, it will never be 100% complete or 100% bulletproof. I can guarantee you that. Life is much more surprising than we can imagine.

Even if you could work out every last detail of your plan, it would probably take so long that by the time you finished it, it would be out of date.

Remedy

Before you object, please do not get me wrong. I am not saying that you should not make careful plans. On the contrary, having a clear plan is an important part of a successful journey. But you also need to recognize when the plan is good enough and ready for execution. So how do you know this? Here are some guidelines.

1. You have clearly identified the end goal and its due date.
2. You have clearly identified the first three steps and their due dates.
3. You have discussed your plan with your significant others.
4. One of the three action points involves consulting others, asking for help. For example, if you want to radically change your career, one of the most important steps is to talk to others who are in that field.
5. You have identified the three main obstacles (internal and external) that could block your path and you have thought of ways to deal with them.

That's it! These are the crucial steps to follow when you want to start a new path. When I was changing my career, my plan looked like this:

1. End goal: become a psychotherapist in five years' time.
2. First important steps:
   Goal #1: Become a coach in a year's time.
   Goal #2: Start coaching practice just after completing studies 1/1/2010.
   Goal #3: Start studies to become psychotherapist 1/1/2010.
3. Yes, I did discuss the plan with my husband and had his full support.
4. I did talk to a good friend who had completed coaching studies. This finally convinced me to go for it.

5. My main obstacle or, rather, constraint was time. I had a young baby so I was worried about whether I would be able to keep up with the lessons and do all the necessary studying. I came to clear agreements with my husband about my study time. He even took a day off (from a very important and busy job) every two weeks to stay home with our daughter so that I could go to my classes.

    I also reached clear agreements with myself regarding study time. I had to study and submit all the papers in Dutch (a newly acquired language) so it took me twice as much time and effort. I studied mostly while my daughter was asleep during the day, but it also took many of my evenings and weekends. But because I loved the subject so much, I never really considered it a real burden or obstacle.

Now it is your turn. If you follow these pointers, is your plan ready? If not, give yourself a week to finish it — then just jump in and start!

This is one of my excuses
Y ( )   N ( )

How do I plan to deal with it?

_____

Empowering Beliefs

I also have good news! Just as there is a saboteur, there are other parts in us, stemming from our Free Child and Adult, which are a source of courage and strength. They also want something from us. Something that is mostly the opposite of what the saboteur wants. This is often why we experience so many inner conflicts. We want something badly yet we are scared to death to do it.

I like to call these other parts "empowerers". Let's take a moment to look closely at who they are and what they want from us. Look at your goal or dream and think of the WHY?, the kind of positive implications it will have on your life, and who you will become, thanks to it.

Marc's story

Marc's dream is to start his own company. His main fears are not being able to take care of his family financially if he gives up his job and follows his dream. He looks his fear in the eye; it is a fear of failure connected with a strong feeling of responsibility for his family. Marc's wife is not working so the family depends entirely on his income. Marc then looks more deeply at the issue and answers this question: what is the worst-case scenario? This would be failing to get any clients and not earning enough to support his family. He realizes that if this happens, he has the option of going back to a full-time job in a corporation. Although that would not be ideal, this thought gives him the courage to quit. Another part of him wants to be free to start focusing on the projects he feels he is good at. He realizes that if he does not try, he will become frustrated, which will also have negative consequences for his family. His Free Child and Critical Parent are clearly in conflict. But when Marc discovers that and looks at his options, he decides to quit and starts working for himself. He realizes that thanks to this decision, he feels free, liberated.

The most important thing to remember is that you have a choice: you can listen to the saboteur or to the empowerer.

Now think about what your empowerer is telling you. What does it want you to accomplish and how is she/he cheering you on to do that?

My "empowerer" tells me:

_____

_____

_____

_____

We call these statements empowering beliefs. These are the beliefs that are in opposition to your limiting beliefs. Now rephrase your limiting beliefs as positive, empowering ones.

Limiting belief 1

_____

_____

I choose to reframe it as the following **empowering belief 1**

_____

_____

Limiting belief 2

_____

_____

I choose to reframe it as the following **empowering belief 2**

_____

_____

Limiting belief 3

_____

_____

I choose to reframe it as the following **empowering belief 3**

_____

_____

Limiting belief 4

_____

_____

I choose to reframe it as the following **empowering belief 4**

_____

_____

Limiting belief 5

_____

_____

I choose to reframe it as the following **empowering belief 5**

_____

_____

The trick is to remind yourself of these positive beliefs every day. If you think of how long you have lived with the negative ones, you cannot expect to fix them after one exercise. Miracles do happen, but if this did not happen for you, please put the statements somewhere visible and read them out loud daily. As they say: "Fake it till you make it" or "Fake it till you believe it and become it."

Repeat them like a mantra. And don't stop after the first few days. Quitting too soon is the biggest mistake people make.

My daily mantra is:

_____

_____

I am going to place it (on my mirror / in my wallet / in my wardrobe / close to my computer...):

_____

How will this change your life?

If you do this consistently, it can have a profound positive impact, not only on your career choice, but also on your entire life.

It can impact your life in numerous ways:
- » You will gain more control over your life.
- » You will be able to do the things you always wanted to.
- » You will do the job that you love.
- » You will become happier and more positive about yourself.
- » You will share your happiness with others.

Clients' Stories

Kasia

"It was eye-opening to realize that I don't have to be a product of my circumstances or to approach my career randomly."

Six years ago, I worked in the enrollment department of a highly esteemed British university. The rewarding part of the job was discovering what motivated prospective students so that I could guide them accordingly. But the other aspect of the job, which was sales oriented, was too pressured, so I wanted to quit.

Even though I wanted to do something related to counseling and coaching to give me the tools and techniques to become better at what I was doing, I felt that the job at the university wasn't the right path for me. My competitive nature, which made me a lioness in sales and enrollment, was changing. I felt drawn to the more supportive professions.

Using my people skills to help and support others to fulfill their potential has been a feature of my entire life, and I enjoy it immensely.

I also felt that I was good at inspiring people. It came naturally, without being forced, and was confirmed by those I helped, in formal and informal ways. So I started to entertain thoughts of starting my own coaching endeavors. I just wasn't sure how and where to start. I already had a few things in place, though: I was motivated and driven to start my own coaching practice; I had an interest and an educational background in psychology; and I was working towards professional qualifications in coaching and counseling.

It was necessary for me to see Dorota for two reasons. Firstly, I needed guidance on how to start my own coaching business, and secondly, I wanted to see what it was like to be a client coached by a professional coach. The situation was a bit tricky as I was about to become Dorota's competitor. Thankfully she didn't see it that way and gave me excellent and genuine support. Big hug, Dorota!

Dorota's coaching fulfilled my need to understand how to shift my career smoothly and start a coaching business so that I could use my skills and natural talents to do something I love.

The coaching gave me the extra push I needed and gave me the tools to put me on the right path. For example, the "Timeline" exercise (page 63) gave me perspective on what I want, not just at present, but five to ten years from now. It was eye-opening to realize that I don't have to be a product of my circumstances or to approach my career randomly. This exercise helped me focus and made me realize that I am in charge — my choices determine what my life will look like. It made me think, "I'd better start doing something today! I want to start what I dream about NOW without any more excuses or postponements... ."

Five years have passed since then and many things have changed. Between 2012 and 2015, I ran a successful coaching practice in Amsterdam, specializing in life and leadership coaching. There were many challenges before I was able to make it a success. It wasn't a walk in the park. I had to hold down my job at the university to maintain a stable income, and I had to negotiate the contract to reduce my working hours to allow more time to start up my practice. And then there were hundreds of baby steps to take: conceptualizing my offering, starting the website and blog, being active on social media platforms, attending networking events, taking marketing and public speaking courses, acquiring clients, retaining them, and building a referral system. At that time, I also ran a positive psychology column in a newspaper dedicated to Polish expats and I wrote a book, *Self-confidence at Work*. All of those smaller and bigger steps brought me more clients. My reputation was growing.

In 2015, I immigrated to Malta, as I had always been attracted to sunny climates. I felt my career was taking shape and that I could easily replicate it there. I secured a job in the IDEA Leadership and

Management Institute as a training manager specializing in coaching and training middle and upper managers to become better coaches.

The paragraph above describes what I had drawn in my "Timeline" exercise five years earlier. Is it a coincidence? No, not at all; training others to become better coaches is where I aspired to be five years after starting my own coaching practice.

My biggest achievement, which was initiated by Dorota's coaching, is the realization that the steps I DECIDE to take, or the steps I decide NOT to take have a significant influence on the quality of my life and career. I simply have to put something in, in order to get something out. So if this takes extra effort and hard work, and causes sleepless nights, why not, as long as I have the end in mind?

And having the end in sight is a good starting point!

Chapter Fifteen

Getting Support

"You're the average of the five people you spend most of your time with."
Jim Rohn

Not so friendly friends

Before we dive into how to build your own cheerleaders' fan club, let's have a look for a moment at the other side of the coin.

Getting support is one of the most crucial aspects of making a change. The bigger the change, the more support you need. Why? One of our primary needs is that of belonging and acceptance. Corresponding to that need is fear — the fear of rejection. Anyone who has spoken in public knows what I am taking about. We fear that others will not accept us. Why is this fear so powerful? The reason is that it is linked to the powerful instinct of "survival". The principal focus of our brain is just one thing: making sure we survive. We cannot survive alone, we need others. So our brain warns us to be aware of the reaction of others by giving us symptoms such as a racing pulse, stomachache and sweaty hands.

When I decided to change my career, my husband fully supported my decision. But the rest of my circle reacted in various ways. Some of my friends were enthusiastic and supportive. Others were bit skeptical: "Why would you want to change your great auditing career and the wonderful travels that go with it for no money, and a long, uncertain path to success?" They could not or did not want to understand.

Many of my clients struggle with the same thing — a lack of support. The more important the relationship — your husband, partner, mother, daughter, best friend — the more important it is to have their support. But a lot of negative feedback even from people who aren't as close to you could lead you to doubt whether you are making the right decision.

Reasons for unsupportive behavior

A lot of my clients find it helpful when I tell them the reasons others might be unsupportive. Here is a list:

1. Your change forces them to confront their own life.

They might ask themselves: "Am I still living the life I want to be living? Am I still in a job that makes me feel excited?" Sometimes they simply do not want to ask these questions — or are just not ready. This is their right. But your right is to follow the new path you have chosen.

2. Your partner might fear that they will have to take sole responsibility for the family.

If it is your partner that is doubting your plans, it might be that he/she is afraid that they will be left to pay the mortgage and other bills.

3. They fear that you are outgrowing them.

This fear is often present in relationships. When one of the partners starts developing and changing, the other can feel threatened. I had couple of female clients whose partners opposed the ideas they had for their new career path. Often the new career path meant that my clients would step up, learn new things, get into better positions, and earn more money. Their partners were afraid that they would become more successful than they were so they sabotaged them. When the sabotage is confrontational, the partner says explicitly: "I do not want you to do that." It might even become threatening: "If you do that, I will leave you." But sabotage can also take a subtle form. In this case, the partner does not outright disagree, but attempts to persuade them, through their behavior or verbally, not to change. This behavior is manipulative and might be successful if the person does not see through it. Examples? Imagine that you have decided to become a nutritionist. To do that, you need to find an appropriate course. But you notice that whenever you sit down in the evening to search the Internet for the right course, your partner finds a great Netflix movie that you've always wanted to watch. Or he/she might tell you a story of a friend of a friend who changed career, started their own business but went bankrupt, had to sell the house, then his wife left him. This subtle sabotage, which is actually manipulation, can be very powerful. So watch out for it.

4. The fear of losing control over you.

Sad but true: not all relationships are partnerships. Sometimes your partner believes that you are his/her property so when you do the things you want to, he or she might lose control over you and in turn lose you. See the next point.

5. The fear of losing you.

This is a tough one. It shows that there is not enough trust in the relationship and it can also indicate that the relationship is not a partnership, but rather a construct where one partner depends on the other to fulfill their needs. Some of my female clients decided to stay at home for couple of years when their children were born. After a while, they started to feel the itch to go back to work and do something for themselves instead of only for the family. They were then confronted by their husbands who were very happy with the situation of having their wife take care of everything at home. It takes enormous courage and faith in yourself to stick to your decision as it might mean that you need to look critically at your relationship and sometimes even decide to leave.

6. Holding on to limiting beliefs.

In Chapter Fourteen I talked about the power of positive and limiting beliefs and the fact that we need consistency in our behavior. And our behavior is rooted in our beliefs and values.

If, for example, your friend or partner has a core belief that "You do not start a new career path after 40," when she/he hears that that is what you are planning to do, they might start to criticize your idea. Their behavior is consistent with their belief. This is also linked to the next point.

7. Being too judgmental and negative.

Your friend may well have a limiting belief but, as a kind and positive person in general, she/he might keep it to herself/himself and say to you, "Wow, it is great that you are doing that." A judgmental, negative person would bombard you with questions and opinions such as, "What a stupid idea. Have you thought about fact that you are already 40?" and "What if you are not successful?" and so on.

8. Jealousy.

Your partner, brother or friend might simply be jealous of you — jealous that you are realizing your dreams and goals and he/she is not. One of my clients told me that her husband said, "It is nice that you want to change your job, but what about me? What about my dreams?"

9. Being too egoistic and egocentric.

Some people simply refuse to support you as it means that in their perception they will be worse off. They feel surpassed, weak and helpless.

The bottom line

You need to realize that most of these issues often have very little to do with you, and everything to do with them. Your friend or partner (or whoever it is) might be projecting their own doubts and unhappiness onto you. But it is their unhappiness, not yours. They need to take responsibility for their own life, career and happiness, just as you need to take responsibility for yours. Of course it is painful. Of course you want others to be happy for you — and perhaps they will be eventually — but you cannot base your life on what they think and feel. You will be lost.

So how do you deal with negativity related to the points above?

1. Communicate how you feel when you receive negative feedback.

We often do not dare say what we feel when we are attacked. Do not react by attacking them, as this is a poor strategy. Instead, state clearly what you feel: "I feel hurt when you criticize my ideas and dreams." Ask your friend or whoever it is for their reason for criticizing you. Ask them in a kind, yet direct way if they are happy in their life/career.

2. Share your ideas with a select group of people.

If you tend to be sensitive to feedback, choose who you share your ideas with carefully — especially in the early phase of your new path when you are not yet sure yourself where you want to go. Particularly at that stage, you want the people around you to support rather than criticize you.

3. If your partner is not supportive, think about what the main reason could be.

Once you have thought this through, sit them down and have a frank discussion. If your partner is worried about the family finances, you need to come up with solutions that keep your goal in the picture. If your partner is afraid of losing you, you need to look more deeply at your relationship. It might be a manifestation of a bigger problem. Either way, you need to talk.

4. Build a new network of supportive, positive people.

Whether you have an existing support network or not, you need to surround yourself with even more positive and supportive people, particularly people in a similar situation — those who aspire to a have a more meaningful career, people who want to be happy, people who are either planning a change or who have successfully made a change. The latter have already done the tough job of following their new career path. They can help you with advice, they can motivate you, they can be your role model for change, they can inspire you, they can give you a kick in the butt when you need it. People in a similar situation to you will make sure that you stick to your plans.

5. Get a coach.

I really think we should all hire a coach at some point or another in our lives. As one of my clients wrote in her story, if you ask your family and friends to help you out with a challenge that you have, the fact that they are emotionally invested in you affects their objectivity, and, furthermore, they give you advice. A coach does not give you advice.

The coach asks you a lot of questions until you find your own answers and solutions. The relationship with your coach is an Adult-Adult type of relationship. Its main goal is to activate your Adult to take responsibility for your own life. The advice from your family and friends often does not work because they mostly give advice from their Parent ego state. Once they start communicating from that state, it goes directly to your Child. Their advice also often reflects their own limitations and fears.

How to choose a good coach?

The profession of coach has become enormously popular in the last 10 years, with coaching courses popping up like mushrooms after rain. So the first point is to check the level of education your coach has attained.

But even more important than their education, in my opinion, is their life experience. If you are looking for a coach to help you to change your career, check if the coach has changed his/her career. If you want your coach to help you to climb a mountain, ask if she/he has done it themselves. It is possible to coach someone without personal experience, but I believe that to be extraordinary as a coach, you need to be a "life change expert" in the field that you are coaching.

The other important factors in your decision are trust and compatibility. Do you feel you can trust your coach? Do you feel that you "click"?

The coaching relationship is a very special one. As a client, you share a lot of very private thoughts and feelings — and this is very necessary if you want to achieve the change you have in mind. The more you trust your coach, the more open you are willing to be.

How to build a support group?

Start with your goal. Do you want to start your own company? Look for social clubs where entrepreneurs meet. Do you want a new position in a company? Find professional networks in your city. Whatever you have decided to do, look for groups where you might meet people who think the way you do.

I have networked in many different groups and discovered which are best for me. You need to do the same; go to many different networking events to find which groups are the best fit for you. Find people who "talk" the same language.

Don't ever be intimidated. I have often heard my clients say, "Oh no, I am not going to join that group. The women there seem very successful and I am not." Although they might well be successful, they are dealing with their own doubts and fears. As they say, "The grass is always greener on the other side." You could start your own group, as I did once. It takes effort, but is a great experience.

Clients' Stories

Catherine

"Finding your place in the world is a lifelong journey — but saying 'I want to be ...' is so empowering."

I grew up in Atlanta, Georgia, but left for San Francisco in 1995, to get in on the dot com craze. In 2009, I moved to Amsterdam to open a new office for the tech company I was working for. After living there for three years, I decided to move back to Atlanta for several reasons — including the financial crisis in Europe and the US, and family issues.

I hadn't lived in Atlanta in 17 years. I wasn't happy there. I had a good job in a corporate environment but I found it stifling after working in tech startups for so long. The tech scene in Atlanta was more corporate and conservative than my experience in San Francisco.

The job itself was particularly trying and I did not feel valued. It seemed as though I spent more time complaining about it than actively looking for a solution.

Also, while the city was more progressive than the rest of the state, it was still relatively conservative in more ways than I expected. I remember, too, not feeling particularly comfortable in Atlanta; it wasn't the kind of place you could easily walk or bike around and the city center didn't feel safe. I had to drive everywhere (hate driving!) and I missed the ease of living in smaller, safer cities like Amsterdam and San Francisco. The standard of living was affordable, the food was excellent, and I had lots of old friends there but it wasn't the lifestyle I wanted. I wasn't especially interested in moving back to San Francisco either because of the cost and intensity of work I would have to put in just to maintain my life there. Amsterdam offered me the work-life balance I wanted and I knew my tech experience would be in demand.

As I began thinking about what moving back to Amsterdam would entail, I started to feel overwhelmed. My mind darted from "Where am I going to live?" to "What am I going to do about my cat?" to "How am I going to pay for this?" I hoped that if I could secure a job in advance, I would stave off some of my more stressful concerns and maybe even get the prospective company to pay for my overseas move! I understood the city was undergoing a revival post financial crisis and would be a different environment to what I had left. I was also reading about the renewed startup scene and felt that if I could get some insights and introductions, I could tap into the best opportunities.

After visiting Amsterdam a number of times over a three-year period, I decided I wanted to move back but felt that I needed to secure a job in advance.

I sought out coaching for two reasons. While I had the desire to leave Atlanta, I wanted to make sure my choice wasn't based solely on emotion. Secondly, it was a big deal to pick up and leave Atlanta two and a half years after moving back from Amsterdam. It was daunting and I felt I could use some support to get this rather large project underway...

My friends and family were not enthusiastic about the prospect of my leaving again, so I was only too happy to ask for and pay for support by way of coaching.

That's when I searched for and found Dorota on LinkedIn. I needed someone to help guide the way.

The coaching process certainly did help. I reclaimed my confidence in what I had to offer — I've had a great career trajectory. But dealing with change through coaching was not necessarily plain sailing. Besides the fact that Dorota and I were in different time zones, which necessitated 6am Skype calls, I got a bit bogged down with the more personal "What do you want?" aspect of the coaching. I had to dig deep to consider why I wanted to go back. It wasn't enough to just want to get out of Atlanta. I spent a lot of time thinking about the kind of life I wanted to live and wrote down the pros and cons of each city and country. I gave a lot of thought to the big WHY and it turned out to be much more about my life than about work. Part of what I was looking for in moving back to Amsterdam was a better work-life balance, which, for me, involved not working some of the time.

The coaching process also taught me that focus is a superpower. One to three hours of daily focus on your challenge can bring radical change to your perspective and situation. I still struggle with focus when there's so much to distract me — Twitter, American politics, my iPhone — but when I activate the focus laser beam, I'm amazed at what I'm able to achieve.

My greatest breakthrough was realizing that I could just go for it — I didn't have to have a job to move back. That seed, incidentally, was planted by someone I met due to Dorota. I got together with Lisa (who turned out to also have been Dorota's client before)[5] for coffee one November afternoon and she suggested that securing a job in advance was not necessary. "Amsterdam is so very entrepreneurial," she said. "Many people here work for themselves, and you've got great experience." Talking to Lisa gave me a different perspective and, ultimately, the courage to just give it a shot.

Once I had made the move, I soon landed a job with a startup accelerator as their communications lead. But after a year and a half, I decided to freelance and explore writing. Today I'm working in content and marketing, and doing creative writing on the side.

Ultimately, I want to pursue creative writing but I still need to make money so I'm working in tech and writing about all kinds of experiences — customer journeys, startup ecosystems across Europe, case studies and so on. Everyone needs content!

I'm getting to travel, ride my bike, and work on projects that interest me. I have a pretty stress-free life.

My advice to others who are feeling stuck in their careers is to try different things. Think about what interests you and find ways of dabbling in them to get a sense of whether you'd like to learn more.

---

5   Lisa's story is also featured in the book on page 180

In 2017, I spent a lot of time volunteering and enjoyed meeting new circles of people. It's really energizing.

I also spent a lot of time networking. (Dorota was great with introductions!) In Atlanta, I met a very generous man who suggested I look at his LinkedIn profile and let him know who I'd like to meet. By the end of the process, I think he had introduced me to 15 people who, in turn, introduced me to 30 more people. I wanted to get a sense of what was happening in the Atlanta job market, to talk about things they were doing, and what I was interested in. I think we're often too afraid to ask for help. But honestly, have you ever thought "Ugh, I don't want to" when someone has asked you for help? No, you haven't. Maybe someone won't answer because they're too busy, but then you just move on. Finally, don't just look for mentors but for sponsors who will actively advocate on your behalf. No matter where you are in your journey, having people on your side is a blessing.

Besides that, I think that any opportunity to reflect inwardly is an opportunity worth taking. It's not easy — in fact, finding your place in the world is a lifelong journey — but saying "I want to be ..." is so empowering. I wish I had done it more often.

Chapter Sixteen

New Habits

*"Successful people aren't born that way.
They become successful by establishing the habit of
doing things unsuccessful people don't like to do.
The successful people don't always like these things
themselves; they just get on and do them."*
William Makepeace Thackeray

Self-discipline

"Dorota, I want [a new job / career path / new business / . . .] very much, but it is too difficult." This is one of the most common sentences I hear from my coaching clients.

In the next section, we will discuss habits, but you cannot establish any new habit — or achieve anything at all in life — without at least a little self-discipline or willpower.

Your story

In which situations have you said, "It is too difficult"? What are you avoiding doing because it might cause some discomfort initially? Get out a piece of paper and write down an example of when you felt something was too difficult but you still went for it and did it. What did you do? How can you use this knowledge to achieve further goals and dreams?

Torn between pleasure and pain

Two powerful forces drive most of our behavior and decision-making: seeking pleasure and avoiding pain. In this quest, our focus is on short-term gains, so we generally choose short-term pleasure over long-term pain or even pleasure. This explains why we keep eating cake while we are on a diet; we opt for the short-term pleasure of a sugar rush over the long-term pain of potential poor health — and even over the long-term pleasure of being slim.

Our tendency to avoid short-term pain also explains why we avoid a difficult aspect of our work when we are trying to achieve an important goal that would bring pleasure in the long term.

This becomes even more nuanced: in the short term, we will always choose to avoid pain above seeking pleasure. This is thanks to the fact that our brain is predominantly focused on survival. Everything else takes second place. Avoiding pain is a basic instinct — it is the way our "reptile brain" tries to save us from harm.

The problem is that all the BIG things we want to achieve in life: a new career, losing weight, sporting prowess, or manifesting dreams are on the other side of pain. This means we have to go through short-term pain to realize our long-term goals in order to get to long-term pleasure.

Choosing new habits

So you have reached the point where you have your career path ready, you have your plan, and you know how to fight your inner demons. It seems you are ready to take off. For many of you it will be enough; for some, not yet.

As US athlete Jim Ryun said, "Motivation is what gets you started. Habit is what keeps you going." Each change requires you to take certain actions like networking, sending out your CV, and creating a business plan. The greater the change, the more actions you will need to take. The trick to sticking to the plan is not a one-off action but consistent actions. And then habit formation comes into play. Habits are the actions you take consistently every day, every week, every month.

It is often very difficult to break old, negative habits such as smoking, drinking, overeating, or compulsive shopping, and relatively difficult to establish positive new habits. Still, establishing positive new habits is essential for the success of your career change project.

I have to admit that I am not always that great at establishing new positive habits. I am, however, quite good at breaking bad ones quickly and easily. A good example is my decision to stop drinking coffee. I used to have at least one or two coffee lattes in the morning. I woke up happy at the idea of immediately treating myself to my milky, foamy, sweet latte. At a certain point, I started having a few health issues. They were not that serious, but serious enough for me to rethink my coffee habit. It was not so much the coffee itself but the milk that I wanted to cut out. Coffee without milk and sugar did not seem very appealing, so I decided to cut the coffee, milk and sugar all at once. I just told myself, "From tomorrow, I am not drinking coffee any longer." And I stopped. It has now been over five years since then. I gave up smoking many years before in the same way.

How did I do it? I made a decision and set the date. I made sure I told the person closest to me, which is my husband. I also realized that if I wanted to be successful, I needed to establish a new (healthy) habit instead.

In the case of my coffee fix, I decided that I wanted to drink green smoothies instead. It also really helped that I had to repeat my decision almost daily, when people asked me to get a coffee with them. I had to say, "No thanks, I quit coffee. I am not a coffee drinker anymore." Establishing a new habit of drinking green smoothies was quite difficult, mainly because it was much more labor intensive than setting up a cup of coffee. But I pushed myself to do it. The first week was the worst. As time went by, I got really hooked on my smoothie and now I couldn't imagine starting my day without it.

But what if the habits that you need to establish are much more challenging than drinking a green smoothie every day?

I can also relate to that, in the writing of this book! After three years of working on it (including the one and a half years when I didn't do anything during my maternity leave in Mexico), I realized that if I was serious about finishing, I needed to develop a consistent habit of working daily. I noticed that I gave myself very convenient and convincing excuses for not working on my book. I was busy with my kids, too tired, busy with my clients, writing my blog articles, cooking, cleaning, and so on. There was always something. I convinced myself that in order to finalize my book I would have to lock myself in a house with a sea view and ONLY then would I be able to do it. One day it hit me that I was simply fooling myself.

I decided I needed to establish a new habit, writing daily, even if it was just a couple of words. And I stuck to it. But before I did that, I read various articles on how great writers completed their masterpieces. Many of them got up at five in the morning or even earlier to work on their book before anyone else was awake. I am definitely not a morning person, so I decided that I would write in the afternoons when my kids were at school and kindergarten, and in the evening when they were asleep. I got addicted to this routine, especially to my evening session. I loved those moments when everyone else was asleep and all was still in the house. I would make a cup of chamomile tea and start typing. I discovered that I could work perfectly well at home during the evening but I was not so successful at writing at home during the day. I was continuously distracted even if no one was around. So I chose to work at the local vegan restaurant where they serve my healthy new addiction, delicious matcha latte — green Japanese matcha tea with almond milk. And with my revised beliefs about what is possible and what is not, and these newly established habits, I completed my first draft in one and a half months. I was very impressed with myself!

I found that an important part of sticking to a new habit is being able to forgive yourself if you don't stick to your plan for one or two days. During the month and a half that I was writing daily, I got sick and could not force myself to write. I felt miserable and just wanted to lie in bed and sleep. It took three days to get better — three days during which I didn't write a thing. On the fourth day, although I felt pretty well physically, I just didn't feel like writing. I was out of my routine and I was trying to pretend that it didn't exist. From past experience, I knew that if I didn't get back to my new habit soon, I would stop. And I definitely didn't want that to happen. So I forced myself to sit at my computer in the evening and write a few paragraphs. The next day it was much easier to return to my writing habit.

Here are some pointers to consider when replacing an old habit with a new one:

1. Make a conscious decision that you want to start a new habit (or stop an old one) and say it out loud.

2. Link a new habit to another positive activity. For example, for me this was writing during the day in my favorite place with a cup of my favorite tea. In this way you reward yourself for your effort.

3. Inform those around you that you are establishing a new habit or quitting an old one and ask for support.

4. In his blog, jamesclear.com, James Clear, an author, photographer and weightlifter who focuses on habits, advises you to integrate the habit into your identity or, in other words, into who you believe you are. If you tell yourself, "I am a smoker," the chances of you quitting are pretty slim — our need for consistency between our identity and behavior applies here too. So if you want to change your career,

you need to convince yourself first, and create a new belief: "I am the type of person who is able to change the course of their life and career."

5. If you get off track, forgive yourself and get back to your newly established habit without further delay. This is crucial.

Now think of any old habits you need to get rid of and new habits you need to develop to kick-start your desired career change.

The old habits I want to give up are:

1. _____
2. _____
3. _____
4. _____
5. _____

My new habits are:

1. _____
2. _____
3. _____
4. _____
5. _____

Chapter Seventeen

Just DoSo!

"It always seems impossible until it's done."
Nelson Mandela

So we have both come to the end of a journey. For me, it is finalizing this book, and for you, it is finding your new purposeful career.

I hope from the bottom of my heart that it is the beginning of a journey rather than the end. I am actually quite sure it is just the start of your path towards a meaningful career!

As a token of appreciation to you for doing all these difficult exercises, for taking a great leap of faith and for having the courage to fight for yourself and change your career, I would like to offer you an opportunity.

Please let me know how this book has helped you to change your life and career. Send your story to me, at book@dosocoaching.com, and there's a great chance that you will be featured in the next edition and/ or on my website.

I am sure you read all the personal stories that were included in the book, and were impressed and motivated by them. I want your story to inspire others too. "It always seems impossible until it's done" is my favorite quote from Nelson Mandela. So be an example for others. Be the light you want to see.

YOUR STORY

Bibliography

I Could Do Anything, If I Only Knew What It Was: How to Discover What You Really Want and How to Get It, by Barbara Sher and Barbara Smith

Now, Discover Your Strengths: How to Develop Your Talents and Those of the People You Manage, by Donald O. Clifton and Marcus Buckingham

What Color is Your Parachute? A Practical Manual for Job-hunters and Career-changers, by Richard Bolles

Mindset: How You Can Fulfill Your Potential, by Dr. Carol S. Dweck

The War of Art: Break Through the Blocks and Win Your Inner Creative Battles, by Steven Pressfield

Games People Play: The Psychology of Human Relationships, by Eric Berne, MD

Transactional Analysis in Psychotherapy: A Systematic Individual and Social Psychiatry (English Edition), by Dr. Eric Berne

TA Today: A New Introduction to Transactional Analysis, by Ian Stewart and Vann Joines

Delivering Happiness, by Tony Hsieh

Judgement Detox: Release the Beliefs that Hold you Back from Living a Better Life, by Gabrielle Bernstein

The Universe Has Your Back: How to Feel Safe and Trust Your Life No Matter What, by Gabrielle Bernstein

ACKNOWLEDGMENTS

I would have given up many times when writing and publishing this book if it was not for the amazing support, encouragement and motivation from my wonderful husband, Rogier. Schat, I cannot thank you enough for being there for me in my moments of doubt. You helped me to bring this book to life, starting with the endless conversations we had when I was creating the blueprint, being my sounding board, and then reviewing the book. So thank you!

Secondly, big thanks to my family: to my mum, for setting an example by being deeply passionate about her work; to my dad, from whom I inherited an entrepreneurial spirit; to my sister, who encourages me to realize my dreams and is always there to listen, and to support me.

Deep gratitude goes out to Anna Rich, my phenomenal editor, who tirelessly edited my book over and over again. Also, the book would not have come to life without the great design of Lisa Hall from Lemonberry. Lisa's work was complemented by great collaborations with Cidgem Guven, who did the diagrams; designer Sai from 99designs, who did an amazing job with the cover of the book; photographer Cristina Stoian, who has the amazing gift of bringing out the best in people through her photos; wonderful proofreader Rachel Deloughry; and talented illustrator Samrat Chakraborty. Through their brilliant work, this book came alive.

A special thank you to my clients who kindly permitted me to include their stories and exercises in my book. Thank you, Amanda, Ania, Catherine, Kasia, Lisa, Marieke, N.S., Robert, Vera, Magda, Isabella and Yoli for giving your time to participate in this project and for choosing me to be your coach. Without your stories, this book wouldn't be the same.

Endless words of thanks go to all the reviewers, including my beloved sister and best friend, Kasia, my brother-in-law, Radek, my great neighbor, Kay, as well as Ania and Joanna, who, despite not knowing me, invested their free time in providing me with feedback.

Words of gratitude also go to published authors Bojana, David, Barbara, Rosaria, Piotr and Sophie, who shared their experiences with me; thanks for our many coffees, advice and support!

What is quite special, I realized, is that this book has become a collaboration between people of various nationalities — Polish, Dutch, South African, Indian, American, British, Filipino, Mexican, Turkish, Romanian, Canadian, Chinese, Ukrainian and German, to mention a few.

Finally, thank YOU, my reader! Without you, I couldn't have written this book. You have motivated me to come up with new ideas to write about.

Love,

Dorota

www.ingramcontent.com/pod-product-compliance
Lightning Source LLC
Chambersburg PA
CBHW071545210326
41597CB00019B/3130